Fables, Myths, and Fairy Tales

Writing Lessons in Structure & Style

by
Maria Gerber

STUDENT BOOK

First Edition © January 2008
Institute for Excellence in Writing, L.L.C.

Also by Maria Gerber:

Geography-Based Writing Lessons

Institute for Excellence in Writing
8799 N. 387 Road
Locust Grove, OK 74352
800.856.5815
info@excellenceinwriting.com
www.excellenceinwriting.com

Printed in the United States of America

Accessing Your Download

The purchase of this book entitles its owner to a free download of the optional *Student Resource Notebook e-book* (110 pages*).

To download your complimentary e-book, please follow the directions below:

1. Go to our website, www.excellenceinwriting.com
2. Sign in to your online customer account. If you do not have an account, you will need to create one.
3. After you are logged in, go to this web page: www.excellenceinwriting.com/FMF-E
4. Click on the red download arrow.
5. You will be taken to your File Downloads page. Click on the file name and the e-book will download onto your computer.

Please note: You are free to download and print this e-book resource as many times as needed for use within *your immediate family or classroom*. However, this information is proprietary and we are trusting you to be on your honor not to share it with anyone. Please see the copyright page for further details. Thank you.

*If you would prefer to purchase the *Student Resource Notebook* as a preprinted, spiral-bound book, it is available for $19 at www.excellenceinwriting.com/SRN-B

If you have any difficulty receiving this download after going through the steps above, please call 800.856.5815.

Institute for Excellence in Writing, L.L.C.
8799 N. 387 Road
Locust Grove, OK 74352

Acknowledgements

Thank you, Vic, Becca, Andrew & Julie.
Your loving patience made this possible.

Table of Contents

Introduction

To the student...

This book is for you. It is full of heroes and princesses, knights and funny animals. These characters and stories have been in books for ages. Why is that? They are still around because they help you to know about goodness, beauty and truth. Plus you get to laugh a lot.

Ask for help whenever you need it. Also, many times in the book you will read the words, "Ask your brain questions." Well, with the help you receive and the answers you get out of your brain, you will find GREAT thoughts. Then the lessons will tell you how to write down those great thoughts. What a concept!

To the parent or teacher...

Let us begin again. The Great Literature in this book is here for your children to imitate, and you are their coach extraordinaire. Inspire them and help them through the structures. Add stylistic techniques along the way. The posters are going up on the walls. Keep your *TWSS Syllabus* handy and refer to it often.

Always find something to compliment in your children's writing. You really can edit a composition and hand it back without the lecture. Above all, plant seeds lovingly. Water, watch, and pray.

May the Lord bless & keep you. May God hold you in the palm of His hand.
Sincerely,
Maria Gerber

About Public Speaking

Within these lessons are three public speaking programs: after the fables, after the myths, and at the end of the year. You will want to plan ahead for these programs. Please look at pages 32, 58, and 123.

Every time students tell the stories from their key word outlines, they are practicing speaking in front of others. According to Andrew Pudewa, the **Stage One** Objectives are:

1. to stand in front of a group without wiggling, with hands on the lectern
2. to see their key word outline, which should be written in large print
3. to look down at a line of key words, look up at the audience (or over their heads), and speak a complete sentence communicating the main idea

4. to repeat the process with little delay between sentences
5. to follow the rule, "You may look at your notes and you may speak to your audience, but you may not do both at the same time."

6. to avoid sounds or words such as "uh", "um", "like", "ya know"

Stage Two Objectives are:

1. to use prepared and practiced gestures
2. to move out from behind the lectern
3. to convey slightly longer, more descriptive phrases from the outline (*TWSS Syllabus* 8)

If parents and teachers provide regular opportunities, correct instruction and encouragement, children develop the ability to speak in public. Let us be proactive. This important skill will help our children when they assume leadership roles.

What's a Fable?

Several elements make a story a fable. Fables are usually short. The purpose of a fable is to teach a lesson about ways that people behave. The characters are often animals who act like people. Fables are obviously not true, since animals cannot talk and reason with each other. Sometimes the author states the lesson, or *moral*, at the very end of the fable. Actually, a person can learn what **not** to do, because the things that animals or people do and say in the fables are so silly. Fables teach and entertain us.

A fable is a kind of folk tale. That means that French fables may be different than American fables, since French people have different customs and ideas than Americans. At first people learned fables by word of mouth, but we can read them because someone intelligent wrote them down. Many fables are thousands of years old. Finally, it is pleasant to think that fables change a little bit every time someone tells or writes them. **You** are about to become a real, live author of fables.

The Grasshopper and the Ants

It happened that a colony of ants spent all summer busily collecting provisions. Just as they were going down into their home for the long winter, a cold, starving grasshopper approached. He begged the ants to take him in. Then one curious ant asked the grasshopper where his provisions were. Grasshopper explained that he ate and danced with his friends all summer. He hadn't thought about wintertime at all. All of the ants shook their heads sadly.

Moral: In some instances it is wise to plan ahead.

Lesson 1: Key Words

Your goals are: to find key words in sentences

to retell a fable—in your own words and using only an outline—to another person

1. Read the fable about the grasshopper and the ants (page 4). Then in each sentence of the fable, circle the words that match the words in the outline below. They are called **key words**. Why? It is because they're the important words that tell you what the fable is about.

2. A **key word outline** is a method for taking notes. The purpose of a key word outline is to help you remember the main ideas you are taking notes on.

3. Notice the structure of the key word outline below. A line has no more than three key words. Each line of the outline corresponds to its own sentence in the fable.

4. Next, retell the fable—using only the outline—to another person. How do you do that? You do that by verbally making sentences out of the key words.

Model of a Key Word Outline
The Grasshopper and the Ants

I. ants, collecting, provisions

    1. starving, grasshopper, approached

    2. begged, ants

    3. asked, grasshopper, provisions?

    4. ate, danced, friends

    5. not thought, wintertime

    6. ants, shook heads

    7. moral, plan ahead

The Eagle and the Jackdaw

A mighty eagle swooped down from the heights and seized a lamb. Now a jackdaw, observing the eagle's power, felt jealous. He promptly alighted on a ram. To the jackdaw's surprise, he could not lift the ram. Even worse—his claws became tangled in its fleece. After a shepherd caught the helpless bird, he showed the jackdaw to his children. With a smile their father remarked, "He fancied himself an eagle. But right now I'm sure he remembers that he's a jackdaw."

Moral: You need not compare your abilities to others'. Greater talents may have been given to them.

Lesson 2a: Taking Notes

Your goals are: to take notes on the main ideas in the fable

to retell the fable from your key word outline

1. In each sentence of "The Eagle and the Jackdaw," circle one to three key words that will help you recall the main ideas in the fable. Write the key words on the outline below.

2. Next, using only your outline, retell the fable to another person. That is, verbally make sentences out of the key words.

Key Word Outline
The Eagle and the Jackdaw

I. _____

    1. _____

    2. _____

    3. _____

    4. _____

    5. _____

    6. _____

    7. _____

    8. _____

    9. _____

Lesson 2b: Quality Adjectives & Strong Verbs

Today's lesson is about two types of words that will help you to write in a descriptive style. These words—**quality adjectives** and **strong verbs**—"dress up" your writing. Why do you want to dress up your writing? It's your job to create a mood or give details to your reader, so put in a quality adjective that describes a person, place, thing or idea.

A few adjectives are so weak that they hardly describe at all. Which sentence gives you a more interesting picture in your mind?

A <u>big</u> eagle went down and got a <u>nice</u> lamb.

A <u>mighty</u> eagle went down and got a <u>tender</u> lamb.

Strong verbs are another effective way to dress up your writing. They are the secret to grabbing your reader's interest. Which of these sentences is more action packed?

The jackdaw <u>saw</u> the eagle and then <u>went</u> down to <u>get</u> the ram.

The jackdaw <u>spied</u> the eagle and then <u>darted</u> down to <u>seize</u> the ram.

With your teacher or parent, list quality adjectives and strong verbs that you could use instead of the **banned words**. In the future, you could also reach for a thesaurus when you need to find descriptive words. By substituting quality adjectives and strong verbs for banned words, you will definitely begin to write *with style*.

Banned Words					
~~big~~	~~little~~	~~bad~~	~~good~~	~~nice~~	~~pretty~~
huge	wee	rotten	pleasant	kind	gorgeous
___	___	___	___	___	___
___	___	___	___	___	___
___	___	___	___	___	___
~~get/got~~	~~say/said~~	~~go/went~~	~~eat~~	~~like~~	~~see/look~~
obtain	exclaim	travel	devour	admire	view
___	___	___	___	___	___
___	___	___	___	___	___
___	___	___	___	___	___

The Lion and the Mouse

Once when an immense lion was sleeping, a tiny mouse ran across the beast's majestic face. Rudely awakened, the lion placed his huge paw upon him. Then the mouse cried out, "If you let me live, O King, perhaps I may be able to do a favor for you someday." This idea amused the lion so much that he laughingly freed the mouse. Some time later, hunters trapped the mighty lion and tightly tied him. Just then however, the small mouse passed by. Observing the lion's misfortune, he scampered up to him and quickly gnawed the ropes that bound the King of the Beasts.

Moral: Small friends may prove to be great friends.

Lesson 3a

Your goals are: to identify quality adjectives and strong verbs in
"The Lion and the Mouse"
to insert -ly words correctly into sentences

1. Review quality adjectives and strong verbs (p. 8) with a teacher or parent. Then read "The Lion and the Mouse." Next, together find the quality adjectives and strong verbs in the fable. Underline one of each.

2. With a parent or teacher, take notes on the fable's main ideas by completing the key word outline below.

3. Using only your outline, retell the fable to someone.

Key Word Outline
The Lion and the Mouse

I. _____

    1. _____

    2. _____

    3. _____

    4. _____

    5. _____

    6. _____

    7. _____

Lesson 3b
-ly Words

Today you will discover **-ly words**. They are a clever way to dress up your writing. Words that end in -ly make your strong verbs even more interesting because they help your readers picture the action with sharper detail. Do you notice how the following sentences express very different ideas—just by putting in different -ly words?

The lion <u>laughingly</u> freed the mouse.

The lion <u>carefully</u> freed the mouse.

The lion <u>sympathetically</u> freed the mouse.

With a parent or teacher, what -ly words could you insert into the sentences below? On the next page is a list of some -ly words.

The hunters tied him <u>tightly</u>.

The hunters tied him _____.

The hunters tied him _____.

The hunters tied him _____.

The mouse <u>quickly</u> gnawed the ropes.

The mouse _____ gnawed the ropes.

The mouse _____ gnawed the ropes.

-ly Words

			Add your own:
abruptly	frequently	pleasantly	
admiringly	furiously	possibly	_____
affectionately	generously	powerfully	_____
aimlessly	gleefully	precisely	_____
alertly	graciously	presently	_____
ambivalently	happily	probably	_____
barely	hopefully	promptly	_____
boldly	hopelessly	proudly	_____
bravely	hungrily	quietly	_____
briefly	immediately	quizzically	_____
calmly	joyfully	rapidly	_____
carefully	kindly	regretfully	_____
carelessly	lovingly	regularly	_____
cautiously	loosely	reluctantly	
certainly	meanly	repeatedly	
cleverly	mercifully	sadly	
compassionately	mercilessly	speedily	
coolly	methodically	stubbornly	
delightfully	mockingly	suddenly	
dreamily	naturally	swiftly	
easily	noiselessly	tragically	
excitedly	optimistically	unfortunately	
ferociously	patiently	viciously	
firmly	peacefully	wickedly	
foolishly	perilously	wisely	

Some Impostors—
-ly Adjectives

brotherly	lively
chilly	lonely
curly	lovely
deadly	queenly
friendly	saintly
holy	silly
kingly	ugly

The Four Oxen and the Lioness

A lioness who was quite fierce used to prowl about a field where four oxen lived. Many a time she tried to attack them. Whenever she came near, however, they turned their tails to one another—instinctively forming a circle. Whichever way the lioness approached, she was met by the sharp horns of one of them. Unfortunately, the oxen fell a-quarrelling among themselves. Not thinking, each wandered off to graze alone in a separate corner of the field. Then the lioness attacked them one by one. In a short while she made an end of all four.

Moral: United we stand; divided we fall.

Lesson 4

Your goals are: to find quality adjectives, strong verbs, and -ly words in "The Four Oxen and the Lioness"

to take notes on the main ideas in a fable, creating a key word outline

1. With a teacher or parent, find the quality adjectives, strong verbs and -ly words in the fable. Underline one of each.

2. Take notes on the main ideas in "The Four Oxen and the Lioness."

3. Using only your outline, retell the fable to someone.

Key Word Outline
The Four Oxen and the Lioness

I. _____

    1. _____

    2. _____

    3. _____

    4. _____

    5. _____

    6. _____

    7. _____

    8. _____

The Milkmaid and Her Pail

A slender milkmaid was gracefully walking to market carrying her milk in a pail on her head. As she walked along, she thought about what she would do with the money she would be given for the milk. I'll buy some hens, thought the milkmaid, and each morning they will lay wonderful eggs, which I will sell easily. With the money from the sale of my eggs, I'll buy myself a new hat and material for a lovely frock. Then won't all the young men come up and speak to me! Passing by them, I shall toss my head like this. Proudly the milkmaid tossed her head back. Of course the pail fell and all the milk spilled. The foolish milkmaid had to walk home and tell her mother the sad story.

Moral: Don't count your chickens before they are hatched.

Lesson 5a
Writing from Notes

Your goals are: to find quality adjectives, strong verbs, and -ly words
to follow a composition checklist
to write a version of the fable, with help

1. With a teacher or parent, find the quality adjectives, strong verbs, and -ly words in "The Milkmaid and Her Pail." Underline one of each.

2. Take notes on the fable's main ideas by completing the key word outline below. Then, by looking at your outline, retell the fable to someone.

3. Brainstorm on page 18. Then use your outline and your ideas to rewrite the fable. How can you make sure you meet the minimum requirements for the assignment? Follow the checklist on page 19.

Key Word Outline

I. _____

    1. _____

    2. _____

    3. _____

    4. _____

    5. _____

    6. _____

    7. _____

    8. _____

    9. _____

The Milkmaid and Her Pail

Lesson 5b
Brainstorming for Dress-Ups

Your goals are: to brainstorm for dress-ups with a parent or teacher
to use these dress-ups when you write your own version of
"The Milkmaid and Her Pail"

What **strong verbs** could be synonyms?
<u>walk</u> (home)   <u>sell</u> (eggs)   <u>thought</u> (about money)

What other **-ly words** could you add to your verbs? (See p. 13)
<u>proudly</u>   <u>easily</u>   <u>carefully</u>

What **quality adjectives** could describe these nouns? (See p. 9)
<u>milkmaid</u>   <u>eggs</u>   <u>milk</u>

Composition Checklist

☐ name, date, left & right margins

☐ composition double-spaced

☐ title underlined (italicized if word processed)

☐ dress-ups underlined (one of each)

☐ no banned words

DRESS-UP (middle of sentence; underlined)	I
-ly word	
strong verb	
quality adjective	

Carolyn Boyd
September 7, 2007

The Milkmaid and Her Pail

I. milkmaid, walking, pail
  1. thinking, ∅ , milk
  2. hens, eggs, sell
  3. ∅ , buy, hat, frock
  4. young, men, come
  5. passing, toss, head
  6. milkmaid, tossed, head
  7. pail, milk, spilled
  8. home, mother, story
  9. moral, (count) , chickens

Carolyn Boyd
September 8, 2007

The Milkmaid and Her Pail

A milkmaid was walking to town with a pail of milk on top of her head. She was thinking about the money she would <u>earn</u> from the milk. Then she would buy hens and sell their eggs. With that money, she would buy a <u>fancy</u> hat and a pink frock. Young ~~mit~~ men will come up to me! But when I'm passing I'll just toss my head. The silly milkmaid tossed her head. So the pail full of milk spilled all over. <u>Sadly</u> she walked home and told her mother the story.

Moral: Don't count your chickens before they hatch.

THE FOUR OXEN & THE LIONESS
by
DONNIE

I. LIONESS, PROWL, 4 OXEN
  1. MANY, TIME, ATTACK
  2. TURN, TAILS, FORM ◯
  3. APPROACHED, MET, HORNS
  4. OXEN, QUARRELING AMONG
  5. WANDERED, CORNER, FIELD
  6. ATTACKED, 1 BY 1, END 4
  7. UNITED, ↑ , DIVIDED, ↘

Muskoxen vs. the Grizzly
by
Donnie

A <u>huge</u> grizzly bear <u>prowled</u> around the herd of muskoxen. Many times he tried to attack the newborn calves, but the wooly adults turned their tails to each other and formed a compact circle. Whenever the grizzly approached, the muskoxen met him with their horns <u>which</u> were large and sharp. Eventually one day some silly members of the herd started quarreling. <u>As</u> they argued among themselves, a couple of the calves wandered off and became lost on the frozen Alaskan tundra. The hungry bear <u>easily</u> hunted them down, and that was the end of them.

Moral: United we survive. Divided we're dead meat.

The Fox and the Stork

A fox invited a stork to dinner. Wanting to play a trick, the fox gave his guest soup in a wide, shallow dish. Easily the fox ate the soup, but the stork, who had a pointed beak, left hungry. Invited in return, the fox sat down for a meal with the stork a few days later. Now the stork gave his guest minced-meat, which he served in a tall jar with a narrow mouth. With his long bill, the stork dined from the jar. The fox could only lick the brim. This time it was he who left with an empty stomach. Nevertheless, the fox admitted that he had gotten what he deserved, considering his ill treatment of the stork.

Moral: Do unto others as you would have them do unto you.

Lesson 6a

Key Word Outline
The Fox and the Stork

I. _____

    1. _____

    2. _____

    3. _____

    4. _____

    5. _____

    6. _____

    7. _____

    8. _____

    9. _____

With the outline you've just completed, retell the fable to someone.

Lesson 6b
Brainstorming for Dress-Ups

Your goals are: to brainstorm for dress-ups with a parent or teacher
to use these dress-ups when you write your own version of
"The Fox and the Stork"

What **strong verbs** could be synonyms?
ate   gave

What other **-ly words** could you add to your verbs? (See p. 13)
easily   meanly

What **quality adjectives** could describe these nouns? (See p. 9)

fox   stork   dish   jar

Lesson 6c
The Who/Which Clause

Another tool for dressing up your sentences is the *who/which clause*. This is a group of words that describes or adds details to a noun, like this:

The stork, <u>who</u> had a pointed beak, left hungry.

A who/which clause can also connect ideas. For example:

The stork offered his guest minced-meat. He served it in a tall jar.

The stork offered his guest minced-meat, <u>which</u> he served in a tall jar.

With a parent or teacher, add who/which clauses to these sentences:

The fox served soup in a dish, <u>which</u> _____.

The fox, <u>who</u> _____, got what he deserved.

Can you make up some other sentences with who/which clauses about the fox or the stork? With another person, tell each other your sentences, going back and forth.

From now on, each paragraph you write should contain at least one who/which clause.

Composition Checklist

- ☐ name, date, left & right margins

- ☐ composition double-spaced

- ☐ title underlined (italicized if word processed)

- ☐ dress-ups underlined (one of each)

- ☐ no banned words

DRESS-UP (middle of sentence; underlined)	I
who/which clause	
-ly word	
strong verb	
quality adjective	

The Ass and His Purchaser

A man who wanted to buy an ass got one at a nearby neighbor's farm. Fortunately, he arranged to purchase this ass on a trial basis. Now as soon as they entered the man's stable, the animal chose to stand right next to the greediest, laziest ass of all. When the master saw this, he promptly returned the beast to its former owner.

"Haven't you returned this animal rather hastily?" asked the farmer.

The wise purchaser said that he could easily judge the poor quality of the ass because of the companion he picked for himself.

Moral: A person is known by the company he keeps.

Lesson 7a

Key Word Outline
The Ass and His Purchaser

I. _____

    1. _____

    2. _____

    3. _____

    4. _____

    5. _____

    6. _____

Lesson 7b
Brainstorming for Dress-Ups

Your goals are: to brainstorm for dress-ups with a parent or teacher
to use these dress-ups when you write your own version of
"The Ass and His Purchaser"

What **strong verbs** could you substitute for these banned verbs?

<u>got</u> (an ass)   <u>said</u>

What **quality adjectives** could describe these nouns?

<u>ass</u>   <u>purchaser</u>   <u>farmer</u>   <u>companion</u>

What **who/which clauses** could you add to these sentences?

The man, <u>who</u> _____ ,

bought an ass, <u>which</u> _____ .

The purchaser, <u>who</u> _____ ,

returned the ass, <u>which</u> _____ .

What other **-ly words** could describe these actions?

<u>unfortunately</u> purchased the ass   <u>hastily</u> returned the beast

Name_____

Composition Checklist

☐ name, date, left & right margins

☐ composition double-spaced

☐ title underlined (italicized if word processed)

☐ dress-ups underlined (one of each)

☐ no banned words

DRESS-UP (middle of sentence; underlined)	I
who/which clause	
-ly word	
strong verb	
quality adjective	

Lesson 8

A Fable Festival for Family and Friends

Parents and teachers, a Fable Festival, whether simple or elaborate, will provide memorable moments for students, family and close friends. Planned lovingly, the festival will provide a new opportunity for young students to emerge with self-confidence when they speak in public and will also foster the audience's appreciation of fine classical literature.

Refer to the objectives on page 3 as you're helping the students to speak from their key word outlines. Allow time for rehearsal(s) so they can polish their deliveries.

Here are some ideas:

❖ Illustrate invitations to family and friends.

❖ Some students might enjoy dressing up as characters from the fables that they present.

❖ Play classical music before and after the program.

❖ If students have illustrated fables, display them where your guests can view them.

❖ Ask someone to video or photograph the Fable Festival.

❖ Serve treats after your Fable Festival.

❖ Tentatively announce the next literary event on myths and hold a friendly contest to see who can come up with the cleverest name for that event.

For Parent/Teacher: Suggestions for Unit III Summarizing Myths

❖ Read myths together and discuss in terms of the Story Sequence Chart.

❖ Create an outline by choosing *words that show the story sequence*, not by choosing words from each sentence.

❖ Brainstorm for dress-ups together.

❖ Students don't necessarily have to write from every single outline. Could a student choose his two favorite myths to write? Could half the class write one myth and the other half a different myth?

❖ It would be okay for a student to add a twist to a myth. What might that be like? A variation or a sequel: A variation keeps the conflict of the myth but changes the setting or the characters. A sequel keeps the setting and characters but changes the conflict. Find examples on pages 110–112.

❖ Are you enjoying sharing the literature with your students?

❖ Are they enjoying the writing experiences?

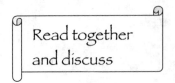

What Are Myths?

Myths of ancient cultures were important for several reasons. Because they dealt with people's sacred beliefs or because they answered questions about cosmic events, myths had a very serious purpose. Some myths also taught lessons about human behaviors. Falling into three categories, many wonderful myths remain important to us even today.

The three categories of classical Greek and Roman myths were creation myths, myths about the gods' activities, and legends about human heroes. The creation myths tried to explain how the world was organized. For example, the reason the sun rose and set was that Apollo, the god of light, drove a fiery chariot across the sky. Other myths told about the immortal King Zeus, his brothers, sisters, wives and children, who each held power over a particular place or action. That was why the Greeks prayed to Demeter for a bountiful harvest, to Athena for success in battle, and so on. Finally, the myth tellers proclaimed legends about heroes who accomplished astounding feats, such as Odysseus who tricked a Cyclops and Hercules who slew a nine-headed Hydra. What impressive drama existed in cultures due to the various kinds of myths!

Amazingly, this drama fascinated people down through the ages, so one can find myths from countless cultures, including Aboriginal, African, American, Arabian, Asian, Egyptian, Iberian, Norse, and Slavic myths. Many myths shaped today's ideas. They are our precious heritage. Myths are essential reading. "We are bound to the past…and it is well to know the old myths in order that we may understand our own times," wrote Max Herzberg in *Myths and Their Meaning*.

Lesson 9a
The Story Sequence Chart

The Story Sequence Chart is a way to outline the sections of a story so that you can write your own version. What are the sections of a story?

Section I introduces the reader to the main **characters**. This section usually gives some background information. It also shows the reader the **setting**, that is, the time and place.

Section II contains the **conflict**, or the problem. The conflict is what the characters need or want. This section shows the reader what the characters think, feel, do, or say to solve the problem.

Section III is usually the most interesting part of the story. The reader finds out the event that solves the problem. That's called the **climax**. Then come the results. The **resolution** shows what happens after the climax. By the end of the story, the characters and the reader have learned a lesson. What is the last line of a fable always named? Yes, the **moral**. Another word for the moral is the **theme** of the story.

Here is the chart about the sequence of stories. Parent or teacher, put the Story Sequence Chart on a wall or the refrigerator for all to see!

Story Sequence

I. **Who** is in the story?
    What are they like?
    When does it happen?
    Where do they live or go?

II. **What** do they need or want?
    What do they think?
    What do they say and do?

III. **How** is the need solved?
    What happens after?
    What is learned?

Create an ending
Title repeats final clincher

Jason and the Argonauts

A handsome hero named Jason and his strong crewmen, the Argonauts, sailed in ancient times across the Aegean Sea to meet the aged King Phineas. Now Zeus, the powerful king of the gods, had blinded Phineas. Zeus also sent three Harpies to torment Phineas. The Harpies were horrible creatures with bodies like birds but faces like ugly old women.

Whenever Phineas tried to eat, they swooped down and violently snatched his food. He was so hungry. So Jason and his men set a trap for the Harpies. Wondrously, two of the Argonauts could fly, because they were sons of the North Wind. They spread a banquet before Phineas.

Then when the Harpies flew down, the brothers took off and chased them far away over the sea. At last Phineas was able to have a meal. He generously rewarded Jason and the Argonauts by telling them many ways to remain safe during their dangerous sea voyages.

Lesson 9b
The Story Sequence Outline

Your goals are: to ask your brain the story sequence questions

to tell the difference between a key word outline and a story sequence outline

to retell the myth using the story sequence outline

1. Read the myth together.
2. Down on the left side of this page are the story sequence questions. On the right side are words that answer the story sequence questions. *They are not words chosen from each sentence.*
3. Ask your brain the questions. Talk about the answers that are given below on the right. Maybe you would have written different answers!
4. Then using the story sequence outline, practice telling the myth to another person. Tell it back and forth several times.

Story Sequence Questions	Story Sequence Outline *Jason and the Argonauts*

I. Characters + Setting
who?
like?
when?
where?
	I. Jason, handsome, hero
	    1. Argonauts, strong, sailors
	    2. Zeus, Phineas, blinded
	    3. Harpies, horrible, bird/hags
	    4. ancient, Aegean Sea

II. Conflict or Problem
what?
want or need?
think? do? say?
	II. Harpies, Phineas, ~~meals~~
	    1. heroes, trap, Harpies
	    2. 2 sons, N. Wind, fly
	    3. set, banquet

III. Climax + Resolution
how?
after?
learned?
	III. brothers, chased, far
	    1. Phineas, eat, lots
	    2. reward, Jason, Argonauts
	    3. tells, safety, voyages
	    4. ~~make~~, Zeus, angry

The Gift of Fire
Abridged from *Old Greek Stories*, by James Baldwin

Prometheus did not care to live amid the clouds on Mount
Olympus, so when the earth was young, he went out among men to
live with them. He found them shivering from the cold.

"If only they had fire," said Prometheus to himself. Then he
went boldly to Zeus and begged him to give fire to men. Zeus refused.
But Prometheus did not give up. He found a reed with a dry center
that would burn for a long time. Prometheus touched the reed to the
flaming chariot that daily crossed the sky. "Mankind shall have fire in
spite of the tyrant who sits on the mountain top!" he declared.

Then he brought fire to the shivering men, showing them how to
warm themselves and build other fires from the embers. After that
Prometheus taught men how to build houses with tools, how to tame
sheep and cattle, and how to farm. They learned to cook their food
and so to eat like men instead of like beasts. They were warm, happy,
and thankful for the wonderful gift of fire.

Lesson 10

Your goals are: to ask your brain questions
to discuss answers with your parent or teacher
to fill in the story sequence outline
to retell the myth using your story sequence outline

1. After you read the myth together, ask your brain the story sequence questions. Do you notice that answers to Section I questions might be in the second paragraph of the myth?

2. Remember to choose *words that show the story sequence*, not words from each sentence. Fill in the story sequence outline together.

3. Now practice telling the myth to another person using your story sequence outline. Tell it back and forth several times.

Story Sequence Questions   *The Gift of Fire*

I. Characters + Setting   I. _____
who?   1. _____
like?   2. _____
when?   3. _____
where?   4. _____

II. Conflict or Problem   II. _____
what want/need?   1. _____
think?   2. _____
say/do?   3. _____
                                     4. _____

III. Climax + Resolution   III. _____
who?   1. _____
like?   2. _____
when?   3. _____
where?   4. _____

The Dreadful Punishment

When Zeus found out that men possessed fire, he got furious.

He mercilessly punished man's helper, Prometheus, for stealing. Zeus

sent Vulcan, the blacksmith god, to chain Prometheus to the rocks on

the highest mountain peak.

There he hung, age after age. Each day an eagle viciously ate

his liver, and each night it grew back. Yet Prometheus bore all his

sufferings without a groan, and never would he ask for mercy or say

that he was sorry for what he had done.

Finally, a great hero named Hercules arrived. In spite of Zeus's

thunderbolts, he climbed the mountain peak. He slew the eagle that

tormented Prometheus. With a mighty blow, Hercules mercifully broke

the chains of Prometheus. The dreadful punishment was over

Lesson 11a

Your goals are: to fill in the story sequence outline with your parent/teacher
to tell someone the myth, using your story sequence outline

The Dreadful Punishment

Characters +
Setting:

I. _____

1. _____

who?
like?
when?
where?

2. _____

3. _____

Conflict:

II. _____

what?

1. _____

want or need?

2. _____

think?

say?

3. _____

do?

4. _____

Climax +
Resolution:

III. _____

1. _____

how?

after?

2. _____

learned?

3. _____

4. _____

The Dreadful Punishment

Lesson 11b
Brainstorming for Dress-Ups

Your goal is: to brainstorm for dress-ups with a parent or teacher

_____

What **strong verbs** could be synonyms?
<u>ate</u> (Prometheus's liver)   <u>asked</u> (for mercy)

_____

What other **-ly words** could you add to your verbs? (See p. 13)
<u>finally</u>   <u>mercilessly</u>   <u>mercifully</u>

_____

What **quality adjectives** could describe these nouns? (See p. 9)
<u>hero</u>   <u>Prometheus</u>   <u>mountain peak</u>

_____

What **who/which clauses** might give your reader interesting details? (p. 25)

Prometheus, <u>who</u> _____,

received a punishment, <u>which</u> _____.

Hercules slew the eagle, <u>which</u> _____.

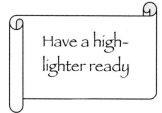

Lesson 11c
The Final Clincher

Your goals are: to highlight 2–3 key words in a final clincher
to brainstorm for a title, with a parent or teacher

Have you ever had difficulty figuring out a title for your story? The way to come up with a creative title is to repeat key words from your *final clincher*.

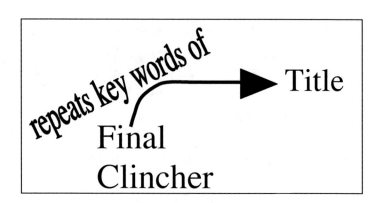

Parent/teacher, this sign on the wall or refrigerator might be helpful.

The title repeats key words of the final clincher. The final clincher is the last sentence in your myth or story. So *after* you write your last sentence, highlight 2–3 key words. Combine them into a title.

The final clincher was: The dreadful punishment was over.
So the title became: *The Dreadful Punishment*

The final clincher was: They were warm, happy, and thankful for the wonderful gift of fire.
So the title became: *The Gift of Fire*

Suppose the final clincher had been: Phineas eats well after the Argonauts ban the Harpies. Ask your brain, "What are the key words?" Now highlight 2–3. Then with a parent or teacher, create a title. It's okay to add words.

Arachne
Abridged from *Old Greek Stories*, by James Baldwin

In ancient Greece a young girl named Arachne was spinning and weaving nicely. She said, "In all the world no yarn or cloth is like mine." Then she looked up and saw in the doorway a tall woman. Her face was fair but stern.

"I am the goddess Athena, and I have heard your boast. Let us both weave. If your work is best, then I will weave no more, but if my work is best, then you shall never use a loom or spindle again." When the day came for the contest, Arachne set up her loom in the shade of a mulberry tree. But Athena set up her loom in the sky.

Arachne wove a web of marvelous beauty. Then Athena began to weave. She took of the sunbeams, and of the clouds and the green fields, and of the autumn woods. Feeling ashamed when she saw this, Arachne cried fearfully, "Oh, how can I live now that I must never again use a loom or spindle?"

Athena took pity on the poor maiden. She changed Arachne into a nimble spider that began merrily to spin and weave a beautiful web. For aught I know, the very next spider you see in a corner may be Arachne herself!

Lesson 12a

Your goals are: to fill in the story sequence outline with your parent/teacher
to tell someone the myth, using your story sequence outline

Arachne

Characters +
Setting:

I. _____

who?
like?
when?
where?

1. _____

2. _____

3. _____

Conflict:

II. _____

what?

1. _____

want or need?

think?

2. _____

say?

3. _____

do?

4. _____

Climax +
Resolution:

III. _____

1. _____

how?

after?

2. _____

learned?

3. _____

Lesson 12b
Brainstorming for Dress-Ups

Your goal is: to brainstorm for dress-ups with a parent or teacher

---

What **strong verbs** could be synonyms?
saw (woman)   said   weave

What other **-ly words** could you add to your verbs? (See p. 13)
nicely   fearfully   merrily

What **quality adjectives** could describe these nouns? (See p. 9)
girl   goddess   web

How might **who/which clauses** be added? (See p. 25)

A tall woman, who _____, spoke to Arachne.

She changed Arachne into a spider, which _____.

Name_____

Composition Checklist

☐   name, date, left & right margins

☐   composition double-spaced

☐   title underlined (italicized if word processed)

☐   dress-ups underlined (one of each)

☐   no banned words

DRESS-UP (middle of sentence; underlined)	I	II	III
who/which clause			
-ly word			
strong verb			
quality adjective			

Title from final clincher (2–3 key words highlighted)   _____

Theseus and the Minotaur
Abridged from *Old Greek Stories*, by James Baldwin

Long ago on the island of Crete, there was a huge maze with

high walls. It was called the Labyrinth. In it were a thousand chambers

and winding ways, and whosoever went even a little way into them

could never find his way out again. In the very center of the Labyrinth

lived the Minotaur, a monster—half man and half bull. Every spring,

seven youths and seven maidens were sacrificed to the Minotaur.

One of these youths was the brave, handsome Theseus.

Now Ariadne, the daughter of King Minos of Crete, planned to

help Theseus kill the fearsome monster, so she secretly gave him a

sharp sword and a ball of silken thread. "As soon as you go into the

Labyrinth," she said, "fasten one end of the thread to the doorpost,

and then unwind it as you go along. When you have slain the

Minotaur, follow the thread back to the door."

Late the next day, the young prisoners deep within the Labyrinth heard a bellowing, very fierce and dreadful. "It is he!" cried Theseus, "And now for the fight!" Down the passage rushed the Minotaur, with sharp horns and fiery eyes and a mouth as large as a lion's. He put his head down and charged forward, bellowing. Theseus leaped quickly aside, made a sharp thrust with his sword as he passed, and hewed off one of the monster's legs above the knee. The Minotaur fell, roaring and beating wildly about with his hoof-like fists, but Theseus thrust the sword into his heart and was nimbly away again before the beast could rise. A great stream of blood gushed from the wound. The Minotaur was dead.

Then the youths and maidens ran to Theseus and thanked him for his great deed. They followed Theseus out of the Labyrinth, past the fearful Minotaur, through the thousand chambers and winding ways, and to the door where the clever Ariadne was waiting joyfully.

Lesson 13a

Your goal is: to fill in the story sequence outline with your parent/teacher

Theseus and the Minotaur

Characters +
Setting:

I. _____

who?
like? 1. _____
when? 2. _____
where?

3. _____

Conflict:

II. _____

what?

want or need? 1. _____

think? 2. _____

say? 3. _____

do? 4. _____

Climax +
Resolution: III. _____

1. _____
how?
after? 2. _____

learned? 3. _____

4. _____

Lesson 13b
Brainstorming for Dress-Ups

Your goal is: to brainstorm for dress-ups with a parent or teacher

What **strong verbs** could be synonyms?
kill (the monster)   said   went (into the maze)

What other **-ly words** could you add to your verbs? (See p. 13)
secretly   quickly   wildly

What **quality adjectives** could describe these characters? (See p. 9)
Minotaur   Theseus   Ariadne

How might **who/which clauses** be added? (See p. 25)

The Labyrinth, which _____

_____, was a maze.

Theseus, who _____

_____, used a sword.

Lesson 13c
The www.asia Clause

Your goals are: to memorize the meaning of www.asia
to correctly add clauses to sentences

The **www.asia** is a terrific dress-up. Are you asking yourself, "What does www.asia mean?" It's an easy way to remember these words:

when   **while**   **where**   **as**   **since**   **if**   **although**

Use these words to start a clause in the middle of a sentence. For example:

They followed Theseus to the door <u>where</u> Ariadne was waiting.

Bellowing <u>as</u> he charged, the Minotaur thundered toward Theseus.

Notice 4 things:

* ❖ the clauses have subjects and verbs in them
* ❖ the clauses aren't complete sentences by themselves
* ❖ the clauses are added into sentences that are already complete
* ❖ the first word of a clause is underlined

With a parent or teacher add www.asia clauses:

A person could never find his way out <u>if</u> _____

_____.

Prisoners in the maze trembled <u>when</u> _____

_____.

From now on put a www.asia clause in every paragraph.

Daedalus and Icarus
Abridged from *Old Greek Stories*, by James Baldwin

King Minos of Crete realized that only the maze-builder Daedalus could have aided Ariadne and Theseus. The vengeful king ordered poor Daedalus and his son Icarus to be imprisoned and guarded deep in the center of the Labyrinth. All through the days Daedalus pretended to be working for the king, but at night he made for himself a pair of strong wings and for Icarus another pair of smaller ones.

One midnight, the two went out to see if they could fly. They fastened the wings to their shoulders with wax and then sprang up into the air. Every fair night after that they practiced with their wings, and then early one morning they flew out of the city. They turned towards the west and headed across the sea for the island named Sicily. All went well for a time, until noon when the sun shone hot.

53

Daedalus called back to Icarus not to fly too high. But the boy was proud of his skill in flying. Said he to himself, "I will go up a little higher. Perhaps I can see the mighty sun master and the horses who pull the sun chariot." So he flew higher and higher.

Pretty soon, however, the heat of the sun began to melt the wax with which the boy's wings were fastened. The wings loosened from Icarus's shoulders. He screamed to his father, but it was too late. Daedalus turned just in time to see Icarus fall headlong into the waves. Daedalus could only look with sorrowing eyes at the unpitying sea, which became known forever as the Icarian Sea after Icarus, the boy who flew too close to the sun.

Labyrinth

Lesson 14a

Your goals are: to fill in the outline and tell the myth to another person

Daedalus and Icarus

Characters +
Setting:

I. _____

who?
like?   1. _____
when?
where?   2. _____

              3. _____

Conflict:

              II. _____
what?

want or need? 1. _____

think?   2. _____

say?
               3. _____
do?

               4. _____

Climax +
Resolution: III. _____

how?   1. _____

after?   2. _____

learned?
               3. _____

               4. _____

Lesson 14b
Brainstorming for Dress-Ups

Your goal is: to brainstorm for dress-ups with a parent or teacher

What **strong verbs** could be synonyms?

see (Icarus fall)   said   flew (higher)

What other **-ly words** could you add to your verbs? (See p. 13)

sadly   proudly   joyfully

What **quality adjectives** could describe these nouns? (See p. 9)

Daedalus   Icarus   wings

How might **who/which clauses** be added? (See p. 25)

The king imprisoned Daedalus, who _____

_____ .

The wings, which _____

_____ , came loose.

What **www.asia clause** could you put in each of the paragraphs? (See p. 52)

56

Name_____

Composition Checklist

☐ name, date, left & right margins

☐ composition double-spaced

☐ title underlined (italicized if word processed)

☐ dress-ups underlined (one of each)

☐ no banned words

DRESS-UP (middle of sentence; underlined)	I	II	III
who/which clause			
-ly word			
strong verb			
quality adjective			
when, while, where, as, since, if, although			

Title from final clincher (2–3 key words highlighted) _____

Lesson 15
Mythical Masterpieces

Parents and teachers, during the past several weeks you provided your students with numerous opportunities to speak from their story sequence outlines. With your continued loving and clear guidance, your children will orally share Mythical Masterpieces during this second program in front of family and friends.

Do your best to guarantee their success. Refer to the objectives on page 3 as you're helping the students to speak from their story sequence outlines. Allow time for rehearsal(s) so they can polish their deliveries. Some children may be ready to progress to more advanced public speaking techniques:

1. Encourage these students to use prepared and practiced gestures.

2. The speaker may move from the lectern as he delivers the complete sentences, first to one side, back to the lectern, then to the other side and back to the lectern.

3. Allow these students to use longer outlines with more than three words per line, so that their complete sentences are more descriptive.

Here are other possibilities:

❖ Some of the Fable Festival ideas (p. 32) might work for this program.

❖ For a game-like segment in the program, practice this mythtelling activity ahead of time: Tell one or two favorite myths sitting in a circle or just close to one another. One person begins a myth and stops after a few sentences. The next person continues, and so on, until the myth ends. The results may be unexpected! The parent/teacher can help students know when to stop and let the next person speak. Experiment to see if they need to hold their story sequence outlines.

For Parent/Teacher: Suggestions for Unit IV Summarizing References

❖ The teaching procedure for this unit will remind you of Unit II.

❖ Students' comprehension of content will increase as you read aloud to them, talk and write **together**. Enjoy the think tank!

❖ Do several outlines together. Children will need help in the skill of **limiting** their note taking. Suggest that they pick *interesting* facts—an appealing idea! They can choose *important* facts later.

❖ At first, they'll summarize one topic from a one-paragraph reference. By the end of this unit they'll summarize one topic from a two-paragraph reference.

❖ For Units IV and VI, create an outline by choosing key words from **facts**, not by choosing words from each sentence. Long sentences might consist of more than one fact.

❖ Students may now go to 4 key words per line on their outlines. Abbreviations, symbols, and numbers don't count as words.

❖ Introduce and emphasize the Topic Sentence/Paragraph Clincher relationship.

❖ In a playful manner, drill students so they memorize the rule, "The topic sentence and the clincher sentence must repeat 2 or 3 key words." Hand gestures help some students memorize. How can you make it a game and laugh as you learn together?

❖ The process is more important than the product.

Aesop the Author

Not many facts are known about Aesop, an author of fables. Oddly, there is a marble statue of Aesop in Paris, France. The sculptor made Aesop's face look ugly. The sculptor also made Aesop look deformed and short, like a dwarf. Why? No one knows what he actually looked like. Aesop spent time in Greece, but it is not certain when or in what cities. In fact, some scholars don't believe he even existed at all. What is known for sure is that someone named Aesop told short tales with characters who were funny animals. These became very popular, and fortunately someone wrote down the tales. Aesop's fables might have been forgotten if they had not been written down. For centuries the world has enjoyed fables by an author named Aesop.

Lesson 16a
Taking Notes From Facts

Your goal is: to compare **notes taken from facts** to notes taken from sentences.

1. Read "Aesop the Author" with a parent or teacher.

2. Discuss the facts that interest you about Aesop.

3. Then read the outline below. Compare the outline to the sentences in the paragraph. Do the key words match?

4. They don't match because the words in the outline are **notes from facts**.

5. During the next lessons, your parent or teacher will help you choose facts and take notes on them.

Aesop, the Author of Fables
by Carolyn

I. T.S. ~~facts~~, author, Aesop, fables
   1. Greece, ~~certain~~, when, cities

   2. scholars, ~~believe~~, existed

   3. short, tales, funny, animals

   4. popular, wrote down

Clincher: *world, fables, author, Aesop*

Lesson 16b
The Topic Sentence & Clincher

Remember these two guidelines when you're writing a paragraph:1) a paragraph is about only 1 topic, and 2) often, the first sentence of a paragraph tells your reader what the topic is.

Topic sentences are general, not detailed, for example:

Not many facts are known about Aesop, an author of fables.

The last sentence of a paragraph—the **clincher**—reminds your reader what the topic was. A clincher repeats 2–3 words of the topic sentence, like this:

For centuries the world has enjoyed fables by the author named Aesop.

Memorize this rule:

**The topic sentence (T.S.) and the clincher sentence
must repeat 2 or 3 key words.**

Study the model below. Then read the paragraph on the next page. With a parent or teacher choose 3–5 interesting facts and take notes on them.

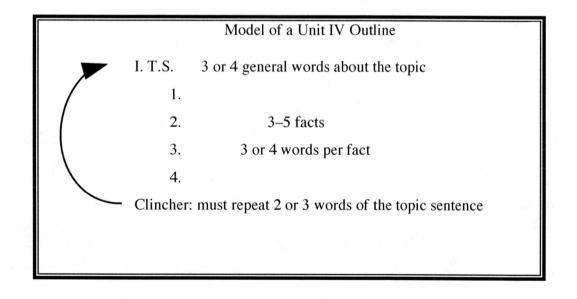

Model of a Unit IV Outline

I. T.S.   3 or 4 general words about the topic

1.

2.   3–5 facts

3.   3 or 4 words per fact

4.

Clincher: must repeat 2 or 3 words of the topic sentence

Aesop—Mixed Up?
by Mark

Facts about Aesop are usually mixed with legends. Some people report that he was a Greek slave who lived in the sixth century B.C. Others claim no such person ever existed. The collection of stories called *Aesop's Fables* are very funny. On this point most readers agree. To them, it's not a serious problem if legends about Aesop are mixed with facts.

I. T.S._____

  1. _____

  2. _____

  3. _____

  4. _____

Clincher: _____

The Brothers Grimm

The Brothers Grimm are famous because of their volumes of fairy tales. Many readers think that the brothers were the authors. Actually, they were wise men who collected and edited the tales. Their collections included "Hansel and Gretel," "Little Red Riding Hood," "Snow White," "The Sleeping Beauty," and many other wonderful tales. Libraries are full of famous fairy tales because of the Brothers Grimm.

Lesson 17a
Limiting Your Notes

Your goals are: to choose 3–5 interesting facts
to take limited notes from the facts, creating an outline
to give a short oral report from your outline

1. With a parent or teacher, read and discuss "The Brothers Grimm."

2. From the paragraph choose 3–5 facts that interest you.

3. Below, write **three or four words per fact**—not per sentence—on a line.

4. It's okay not to take notes from every sentence, because a paragraph has a limited number of ideas in it. Remember the topic sentence/clincher rule.

5. Find a partner and take turns telling each other about the facts.

I. T.S._____

   1. _____

   2. _____

   3. _____

   4. _____

   5. _____

Clincher: _____

Family Ties

The Brothers Grimm grew up in a family with strong ties. Their parents taught them to work cooperatively and take care of each other. Jacob and Wilhelm always attended the same schools as they were growing up. These brothers, who lived together all their lives—even after Wilhelm married—were obviously devoted to each other. Laboring productively for over forty years, together they collected and published great fairy tales for others' enjoyment. Truly, the loving family ties of the Brothers Grimm benefited millions.

Lesson 17b

Your goals are: to choose 3–5 interesting facts from the paragraph above

to take limited notes from the facts, creating an outline

1. With a parent or teacher, read and talk about "Family Ties."

2. Choose 3–5 facts. Do you see that long sentences might have 2 facts in them?

3. Below, write three or four words per fact—not per sentence—on a line. It's okay not to include every sentence. Limit your notes. Remember the topic sentence/clincher rule (p. 63).

4. Find a partner and take turns telling each other about the facts.

I. T.S._____

   1. _____

   2. _____

   3. _____

   4. _____

   5. _____

Clincher: _____

Lesson 17c
Brainstorming for Ideas

Your goals are: to brainstorm for ideas with a parent or teacher

What are your general key words for a **topic sentence**?

_____

What **strong verbs** will grab your reader's interest?

_____

What **-ly words** will you add to your verbs? (See p. 13)

_____

What **quality adjectives** might describe these nouns? (See p. 9)
brothers   family   fairy tales

_____

What **who/which clause** will give your reader details? (See p. 25)

_____

What **www.asia clause** might you put in the paragraph? (See p. 52)

_____

What might your **clincher** be? Repeat 2 or 3 words from the topic sentence.

Now you're ready to write 1 paragraph from your outline (p. 66).
Use the checklist on the next page to help you meet the minimum requirements.

Name _____

Composition Checklist

☐   name, date, left & right margins

☐   composition double-spaced

☐   Title is underlined (italicized if word processed).

☐   Dress-ups are underlined (one of each).

☐   no banned words

Clear topic sentence (key words highlighted)   _____

DRESS-UP (middle of sentence; underlined)	I
who/which clause	
-ly word	
strong verb	
quality adjective	
when, while, where, as, since, if, although	

Clear clincher (repeats 2 or 3 highlighted words of T.S.)   _____

Title (repeats 2 or 3 words of clincher)   _____

Influencing Hans Christian Andersen

The family of Hans Christian Andersen strongly influenced his life's work—writing. Evidently Hans Christian's grandmother told him old European fairy tales. While making shoes, his father dreamed of being a wealthy gentleman. He firmly impressed on his son that he must lift himself out of poverty and ignorance. His mother, who became a washerwoman after Hans Christian's father died, sacrificed for him. These influential family members contributed to Hans Christian's writing potential.

His writing was also affected by experiences in his youth—some joyful, some miserable. Hans Christian loved literature. As he recited Shakespearean plays by heart, he put on clever puppet shows. At home that kind of creativity was encouraged. Cruelly ridiculed at school, however, Hans Christian was often humiliated by other boys. Later he wrote about how that felt in his fairy tale "The Ugly Duckling." When he was fourteen years old, several adults who noticed Hans Christian helped him to begin his career. The strong influence of his family plus powerful early experiences helped produce the wonderful writings of Hans Christian Andersen.

Lesson 18a
Summarizing from Two Paragraphs

Your goals are: to take limited notes from facts, creating an outline

to give a short oral report from your outline

1. With a parent or teacher, read and discuss page 69.

2. Choose 4–6 facts **out of the entire page** that interest you. You won't be able to take notes from every sentence.

3. Below, write three or four words per fact—not per sentence—on a line. Remember the topic sentence/clincher rule (p. 63).

4. Find a partner and take turns telling each other about the facts.

I. T.S._____

    1. _____

    2. _____

    3. _____

    4. _____

    5. _____

    6. _____

Clincher:

Lesson 18b
Brainstorming for Ideas

Your goals are: to brainstorm for ideas with a parent or teacher

What are your general key words for a **topic sentence**?

What **strong verbs** will grab your reader's interest?

What **-ly words** will you add to your verbs? (See p. 13)

What **quality adjectives** might describe these nouns? (See p. 9)
<u>family</u>   <u>father</u>   <u>experiences</u>

What **who/which clause** will give your reader details? (See p. 25)

What **www.asia clause** might you put in the paragraph? (See p. 52)

What might your clincher be? Repeat 2 or 3 words from the topic sentence.

Now you're ready to write 1 paragraph from your outline (p. 70).
Use the checklist to help you meet the minimum requirements.

71

Name_____

Composition Checklist

<table>
<tr><td>❏</td><td>name, date, left & right margins</td></tr>
<tr><td>❏</td><td>composition double-spaced</td></tr>
<tr><td>❏</td><td>Title is underlined (italicized if word processed).</td></tr>
<tr><td>❏</td><td>Dress-ups are underlined (one of each).</td></tr>
<tr><td>❏</td><td>no banned words</td></tr>
</table>

Clear topic sentence (key words highlighted) _____

DRESS-UP (middle of sentence; underlined)	I
who/which clause	
-ly word	
strong verb	
quality adjective	
when, while, where, as, since, if, although	

Clear clincher (repeats 2 or 3 highlighted words of T.S.) _____

Title (repeats 2 or 3 words of clincher) _____

Influences on Hans Christian Andersen
by Victor

I. T.S. family, H.C. Andersen, influenced, writing

   1. grandmother, told, father, dreamed

   2. mother, washerwoman, sacrificed

   3. experiences, youth, joyful, miserable

   4. home, encouraged, school, humiliated

   5. wrote, "Ugly Duckling"

Clincher: H.C. Andersen, influence, family, experiences

Influences on Hans Christian Andersen
by Victor

The fantastic writings of Hans Christian Andersen were influenced by his family. Growing up with his grandmother, who told him old European folk tales, and his father, who dreamed of becoming a fancy gentleman, Hans Christian chose a writing career. In one of his most sensitive fairy tales, "The Little Matchgirl," perhaps Hans Christian was thinking of his dear mother, because when she was a child she was very poor. In addition to the influence of his family, memorable experiences from Hans Christian's youth affected what he wrote about. Some were joyful. Some were miserable. For example, Hans Christian was lovingly encouraged at home, but at school the other boys humiliated him. Did he write "The Ugly Duckling" about himself? How wonderfully his family and experiences influenced the great writings of Hans Christian Andersen.

For Parent/Teacher: Suggestions for Unit V Writing from Pictures

❖ The three fairy tales for this unit, as well as Internet links for other public domain literature, can be found in the Appendix. How about reading aloud four days a week?

❖ Please recall that you have flexibility with the source texts and lessons. The three fairy tales for this unit were chosen for their familiarity, but you could use others.

❖ An optional lesson on past perfect tense is on pages 84–85. Past perfect tense is useful in Unit V, which is basically **event description**.

❖ Students don't necessarily have to write from every single outline. Could a student choose his favorite fairy tale to write? Could part of the class write from one series of pictures, another part from a different series, and so on?

❖ Do several outlines together. Put up the Writing from Pictures chart (p. 75). It lists the questions they'll be asking themselves.

❖ Students may still write up to 4 key words per line on their outlines. Abbreviations, symbols, and numbers don't count as words.

❖ In this unit, the topic sentence = the central fact (what is happening) in the picture.

❖ Have students add 2 words to the rule they memorized: "The topic sentence and the clincher sentence must repeat **or reflect** 2 or 3 key words."

❖ Younger students, who might have difficulty constructing clinchers that "reflect" the central fact, may repeat the topic sentence exactly and then rewrite with a synonym.

❖ Are you looking ahead to Unit VII? There, the children will have an opportunity to create original fables, myths and fairy tales. Today, take a moment to ask your brain, "Am I preparing them to **think** about how to do that? Do they have enough stories in their heads?"

Writing from Pictures

Title (from Final Clincher)

I.   Topic Sentence=Central Fact of Picture 1

What are the characters thinking and feeling?

What had happened just before?

(May require past perfect tense; use "had" + action verb.)

Why did it happen?

What is happening around the scene?

Clincher (Repeat or reflect 2 or 3 words of Central Fact.)

II. Topic Sentence=Central Fact of Picture 2

What are the characters doing, thinking and saying?

How do they feel? How are they showing their feelings?

What is happening around the scene?

Why?

Clincher (Repeat or reflect 2 or 3 words of Central Fact.)

III. Topic Sentence=Central Fact of Picture 3

What are the characters doing, thinking and saying?

How do they feel? How are they showing their feelings?

What is happening around the scene?

What will happen next? Was there a lesson?

Clincher (Repeat or reflect 2 or 3 words of Central Fact.)

Why Are They Called Fairy Tales?

Stories that are called fairy tales have several features in common. Many of them begin with the famous words "Once upon a time," and many of them happen long ago in a faraway kingdom with deep forests or beautiful palaces. These tales always reveal a problem that needs to be solved by characters such as princes and princesses, fairies, elves and talking beasts. Usually, the writer clearly shows the "good guys" who are against the "bad guys," but most of the fantastic events in fairy tales could never happen in real life. For example, Jack couldn't really climb a beanstalk up into the clouds to find a goose that lays golden eggs. Teaching a lesson or having a theme, a fairy tale can be educational as well as entertaining. Did your parent ever warn you not to talk to strangers? That's what the mother tries to teach her daughter in "Little Red Riding Hood." Finally, the story might end with the famous words "...and they all lived happily ever after." In conclusion, although fairy tales may come from countries you've never visited, the features they have in common make them seem like familiar friends.

Lessons 19, 20, 21
Writing from Pictures

For the next three lessons (or as many as your parent/teacher wants), write stories that are three paragraphs long. Instead of taking notes from sentences or facts, write about what you see happening in a comic. Here's how:

1. With a parent or teacher, look at the top picture on page 78. On the first line, in 3–4 key word notes, write what you see happening. This is **the central fact**. The topic sentence = the central fact.

2. Next, ask your brain questions like:

What are the characters thinking and feeling?

What had happened just before?[*] Why did it happen?

What is happening around the scene?

Answer your questions in 3–4 key word notes per line.

3. End the first paragraph. Follow the rule: The topic sentence and the clincher sentence must repeat **or reflect** 2–3 key words. Highlight the key words you repeat or reflect. "Reflect" means find a synonym. Do the same for the second and third paragraphs. Toward the end of the third paragraph, ask your brain, "What will happen next? Was there a lesson?"

4. The final clincher must repeat or reflect 2–3 key words from the central fact of the last paragraph. The title must repeat or reflect the highlighted 2–3 key words from the final clincher. (See chart p. 75.)

---

[*] optional lesson on past perfect tense, pp. 84–85

Cinderella

I. Central fact:_____

_____

_____

_____

_____

Clincher:_____

II. Central fact:_____

_____

_____

_____

_____

Clincher:_____

III. Central fact:_____

_____

_____

_____

_____

Clincher:_____

Name_____

Composition Checklist

- ☐ name, date, left & right margins

- ☐ composition double-spaced

- ☐ title underlined (italicized if word processed)

- ☐ dress-ups underlined (one of each)

- ☐ no banned words

DRESS-UP (middle of sentence; underlined)	I	II	III
who/which clause			
-ly word			
strong verb			
quality adjective			
when, while, where, as, since, if, although			

Central fact (2–3 key words highlighted)   _____

Title from final clincher (2–3 key words highlighted)   _____

Clincher reflects central fact (2–3 key words highlighted)   _____

Beauty and the Beast

I. Central fact:_____

_____

_____

_____

_____

Clincher:_____

II. Central fact:_____

_____

_____

_____

_____

Clincher:_____

III. Central fact:_____

_____

_____

_____

_____

Clincher:_____

Name_____

Composition Checklist

❒	name, date, left & right margins
❒	composition double-spaced
❒	title underlined (italicized if word processed)
❒	dress-ups underlined (one of each)
❒	no banned words

DRESS-UP (middle of sentence; underlined)	I	II	III
who/which clause			
-ly word			
strong verb			
quality adjective			
when, while, where, as, since, if, although			

Central fact (2–3 key words highlighted)   _____

Title from final clincher (2–3 key words highlighted)   _____

Clincher reflects central fact (2–3 key words highlighted)   _____

I. Central fact:_____

_____

_____

_____

_____

Clincher:_____

II. Central fact:_____

_____

_____

_____

_____

Clincher:_____

III. Central fact:_____

_____

_____

_____

_____

Clincher:_____

Name_____

Composition Checklist

- ☐ name, date, left & right margins
- ☐ composition double-spaced
- ☐ title underlined (italicized if word processed)
- ☐ dress-ups underlined (one of each)
- ☐ no banned words

DRESS-UP (middle of sentence; underlined)	I	II	III
who/which clause			
-ly word			
strong verb			
quality adjective			
when, while, where, as, since, if, although			

Central fact (2–3 key words highlighted) _____

Title from final clincher (2–3 key words highlighted) _____

Clincher reflects central fact (2–3 key words highlighted _____

Optional Lesson 21b
The Past Perfect Tense

When you write from pictures, you're describing events. Use the past perfect tense to describe an event that happened **before another event in the past**. "The past" might have been ten minutes ago, yesterday, last week, or a long time ago.

Examples:

When she <u>had finished</u> her work, Cinderella used to go into the chimney-corner.

That sentence tells you that in the past, Cinderella used to go into the chimney-corner, but even before she went there, she finished her work.

Cinderella thanked her godmother for the dress because the prince <u>had admired</u> it at the ball.

That sentence tells you that in the past—maybe five minutes ago—Cinderella thanked her godmother. Earlier than that—perhaps an hour ago—the prince admired her dress.

Did you notice the underlined words? The pattern of the past perfect tense is:

<u>had</u> + <u>action verb</u>

Cinderella's stepsisters begged forgiveness for the mean things they <u>had done</u> to her.

The Past Perfect Tense, cont.

With a parent or teacher, how many sentences can you make up that use the past perfect tense? For example:

Cinderella handed her stepsisters oranges that the prince had given to her.

The stepsisters reported that the prince had danced all night with a beautiful princess.

The Beautiful Princess's Slipper

by  Therese

Once upon a time a prince met the most beautiful princess in his kingdom. He thought she was charming, and when others asked her to dance, the prince quickly announced, "She's my partner." The princess, whose name was Cinderella, felt honored. Her stepsisters were jealous. Cindi's fairy godmother had poofed up a gown and a carriage, which went fast. When Cindi arrived, the crowd whispered, "Who is she?" At the end of the night, the prince hoped he'd see the beautiful princess again.

The next time Cindi attended the ball, she forgot that the magic would end at midnight, and had to flee the palace. "I must go! The time!" she cried. Cindi madly raced down the stairway as her gown turned to rags. One of the slippers which her godmother had given her fell off. The prince watched as Cindi ran from the palace, and he vowed he'd find her.

Ordered by the prince, a courteous manservant walked around the kingdom trying the slipper on all the princesses and lovely maidens. The slipper didn't fit the stepsisters, when suddenly Cindi asked, "May I try?" The slipper fit like a glove, and Cindi pulled the other out of her pocket. While the amazed stepsisters watched, Fairy Godmother poofed Cindi into the best gown yet. The prince married Cindi, who kindly allowed her stepsisters to live in the palace. The lesson to all princesses is, when the slipper fits, wear it!

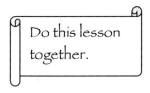

Do this lesson together.

Lesson 22a
The Fused Outline*

Your goals are: given 2 paragraphs, to choose 4–6 facts *from each*

to take limited notes from the facts, creating 2 outlines

to fuse 2 outlines into 1

1. Read and discuss "Daedalus and Icarus Escape Again" (p. 88).

2. From the paragraph choose 4–6 interesting facts.

3. On page 89 create an outline by writing three or four words **per fact**—not per sentence—on the lines.

4. Remember, it's okay not to take notes from every sentence.

5. Repeat steps 1–3 with "Night Crossing." This time choose different facts.

6. Now you have 2 outlines on the same topic. What would you say the topic is? **Fuse**—that means melt—some of the facts from each outline into one. This fused outline will have 5–7 notes, plus 2 or 3 key words for a topic sentence and for a clincher sentence. (See p. 77 to review the rule.)

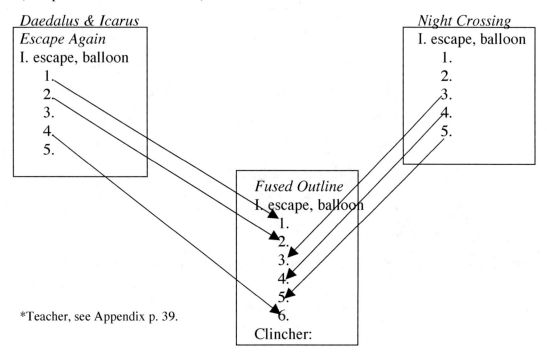

*Teacher, see Appendix p. 39.

Daedalus and Icarus Escape Again

Peter Strelzyk's and Gunter Wetzel's escape from Communist East Germany in a hot air balloon sounds like the myth about Daedalus and Icarus. In 1979 they and their families, who were desperate for freedom, flew over the Berlin Wall. For two years, Strelzyk and Wetzel had secretly put everything together. Then they lifted off and sailed 8,200 feet above the cruel, barbed wire and concrete wall. When they landed on the other side, they were in free West Germany. Truly, they were like Daedalus and Icarus taking flight again, but this time the escape was successful for all.

Night Crossing

One of the greatest escapes in history happened the night that Peter Strelzyk and Gunter Wetzel crossed from East to West Germany in a homemade hot air balloon. They successfully piloted it over the twelve-foot high barrier known as the "Iron Curtain." It was dangerous. They feared that neighbors would turn them in to the police, and there was danger of fire. Secretly, their wives sewed sheets and curtains together for the balloon, while Strelzyk and Wetzel built the basket, a flamethrower and a gas burner. In spite of danger, these eight Germans who risked their lives to flee from the terrors of Communism crossed into freedom one blessed night.

Outline From Facts – *Daedalus and Icarus Escape Again*

1. _____
2. _____
3. _____
4. _____
5. _____
6. _____

Outline From Facts – *Night Crossing*

1. _____
2. _____
3. _____
4. _____
5. _____
6. _____

Fused Outline

I. (T.S.) _____

   1. _____
   2. _____
   3. _____
   4. _____
   5. _____
   6. _____
   7. _____

Clincher _____

Student Sample

Outlines From Facts

Daedalus and Icarus Escape Again

I. escape, hot, O_2, balloon
 1. Peter Strelzyk, Gunter Wetzel
 2. 1979, flew, Berlin Wall
 3. 2 years, put together
 4. landed, free, W. Germany
 5. Daedalus, Icarus, successful

Night Crossing

I. escape, hot, O_2, balloon
 1. night, E. ➡ W. Germany
 2. 12 ft., "Iron Curtain"
 3. feared, neighbors, fire
 4. wives, sheets, curtains
 5. basket, flamethrow, burner
 6. 8 risk, lives, terror, Comm.

Fused Outline
I. D., I., escaped, ~~balloon~~
 1. P. Strelzyk, G. Wetzel
 2. flew, Berlin Wall, 1979
 3. feared, neighbors, fire
 4. wives, sheets, curtains
 5. basket, flamethrow, burner
 6. landed, free, W. Germany
 7. 8 risk, lives, terror, Comm.
Clincher: D., I., escape + title

Daedalus's and Icarus's New Escape
by
Mario

    In the myth, **Daedalus** and **Icarus escaped**, but not in a hot air balloon. In real life, Peter Strelzyk and Gunter Wetzel escaped when they flew right over the Berlin Wall. It was 1979. Fearlessly, they worked in spite of sneaky neighbors and the danger of fire. Cleverly their wives sewed sheets and curtains together to make the huge balloon. Everything worked! They landed in West Germany. The eight people had risked their lives to be free of the Communists' terrorism. The successful **escape** of the new **Daedalus** and **Icarus**—Strelzyk and Wetzel—was glorious and inspiring.

90

Lesson 22b
The -ly Sentence Opener

Your goals are: to start sentences with -ly words

to indicate the -ly sentence opener

You have already learned to dress up your writing by using an -ly word in the middle of your sentences. In this lesson, you'll think of -ly words to start sentences with. Don't underline an **-ly sentence opener**. However, show that you're using an -ly sentence opener by putting a number 3 in the left margin.

With your parent or teacher read the examples below. Then write more sentences of your own that start with -ly words about the escape in the balloon. There is an -ly word list on page 13. If possible, put an -ly sentence opener in every paragraph you write from now on.

3 Carefully, Strelzyk and Wetzel experimented in the basement.

3 Gracefully, the hot air balloon flew over the Communists' heads.

Lessons 23a, b, c*

1. With your parent or teacher, follow the process you learned on p. 87.

2. Find a partner. Take turns telling each other the facts from your outlines.

3. On page 95 you can brainstorm for ideas with an adult.

4. Together, write **one** paragraph from your fused outline. Use the checklist to help you meet the minimum requirements.

The Knights of the Round Table

There are many legends about the group of men called the Knights of the Round Table. Obviously, this was the group's title because they made plans at a great round table. The legends told about each knight and how he promised to serve Arthur, the King of England. These knights also vowed to follow a code: to aid any lady who asked for help, to protect the weak and innocent, to fight evildoers and to defend each other courageously. People of all ages enjoy legends about the brotherhood of warriors known as the Knights of the Round Table.

*Note to Parent/Teacher: For an enjoyable prelude to these next lessons, read aloud *The Sword in the Stone*. It can be found in the Appendix on page A-32.

Lessons from the Round Table Knights

Through the centuries, legends about the Round Table Knights have been important because they have taught many lessons about valor and loyalty. Since the knights' great table had a round shape, it signified equality among the knights. From this, people learned the importance of humbly respecting others. The fact that the knights vowed to defend each other inspired people to practice loyalty and unselfishness. Finally, although the knights were very powerful—able to destroy their enemies—they assisted helpless women and children. By these actions, they showed others how to be merciful. Clearly, the legends about the virtues of the Knights of the Round Table can still teach us today.

Outline From Facts – *The Knights of the Round Table*

1. _____
2. _____
3. _____
4. _____
5. _____
6. _____

Outline From Facts – *Lessons from the Round Table Knights*

1. _____
2. _____
3. _____
4. _____
5. _____
6. _____

Fused Outline

I. (T.S.) _____

    1. _____

    2. _____

    3. _____

    4. _____

    5. _____

    6. _____

    7. _____

Clincher _____

Brainstorming for Ideas

Your goal is: to brainstorm for ideas with a parent or teacher

What are your general key words for a **topic sentence**?

_____

What **strong verbs** will grab your reader's interest?

_____

What **-ly words** will you add to your verbs? (See p. 13)

_____

What **quality adjectives** might describe these nouns? (See p. 9)
knights   legends   king

_____

What **who/which clause** will give your reader details? (See p. 25)

_____

What **www.asia clause** might you put in the paragraph? (See p. 52)

_____

What **-ly sentence openers** will add variety to your sentences? (See p. 91)

Composition Checklist

☐   name, date, left & right margins

☐   composition double-spaced

☐   title underlined (italicized if word processed)

☐   dress-ups underlined (one of each)

☐   sentence openers marked in margin

☐   no banned words

Clear topic sentence (key words highlighted)   _____

DRESS-UP (middle of sentence; underlined)	I
who/which clause	
-ly word	
strong verb	
quality adjective	
when, while, where, as, since, if, although	

OPENERS (first word of sentence; number in margin)	I
❸ -ly	

Clear clincher (repeats 2 or 3 highlighted words of T.S.)   _____

Title (repeats 2 or 3 words of clincher)   _____

Lessons 24a, b, c

Perhaps it still works well for you to outline together, or maybe your parent or teacher will let you work on your own for a time.

1. **Several times**, read this page and page 98.
2. Follow the process you learned on page 87.

The Legends of King Arthur

The tales of King Arthur are legends. That means that some parts are true while other parts are commonly accepted but can't be proven. Arthur may be based on a real warrior who fought against the invaders of England during the sixth century. Because he was such a hero, the wandering minstrels and storytellers spread stories about Arthur. These stories became more and more fantastic, and at some point Arthur the hero became Arthur the king. The songs and stories also told about Merlin, the magician who helped Arthur in a peaceful kingdom called Camelot. It was near this place that the king and his Knights of the Round Table battled enemies and traveled, doing good deeds. A great many stories about these characters delighted the people. Consequently, the legends and myths about King Arthur are some of the greatest stories in all of British literature.

Wonderful Tales of Arthur

Tales about King Arthur are wonderful. Probably the best-known tale about him is *The Sword in the Stone*. The stories about Merlin the wizard are also very popular. If they are romantic, some girls eagerly read the legend about the golden-haired Sir Galahad, who was the purest of the Knights of the Round Table. To most of the people of England, however, King Arthur was the true superhero. Supposedly, he will return at a time when they need him most. It is astonishing that so many tales of Arthur came down to us.

History Mixed with Myth

In the literature about King Arthur, history mixed with myth. This combination strongly affected the British people. Although no one can prove Arthur really existed, he is based on a chieftain who battled England's enemies after the Roman troops left. For centuries after Arthur's legend spread, British kings and queens tried to claim the throne by saying they were related to Arthur. Some British people are waiting for King Arthur to return, since one myth said that he never died. This is why Arthur is known as "the once and future king." Possibly myth will mix with history again—so they think.

Outline From Facts – *The Legends of King Arthur*

1. _____
2. _____
3. _____
4. _____
5. _____
6. _____

Outline From Facts – *Wonderful Tales of Arthur*

1. _____
2. _____
3. _____
4. _____
5. _____
6. _____

Outline From Facts – *History Mixed with Myth*

1. _____
2. _____
3. _____
4. _____
5. _____
6. _____

Fused Outline

Your goal is: to fuse 3 outlines into 1 outline

1. What was the topic of the 3 paragraphs you read on pages 97 and 98?

2. Decide on 2 or 3 key words for your topic sentence.

3. Choose *a total of 5–7 different notes* from the outlines on p. 99.

4. **Fuse** them into the outline below.

5. The topic sentence and the clincher sentence must repeat or reflect 2 or 3 key words.

6. Find a partner. Take turns telling each other the facts from your outlines.

7. You can brainstorm for ideas on the next page.

8. When your parent or teacher tells you, write **one** paragraph from your fused outline and brainstormed ideas. Use the checklist to help you meet the minimum requirements.

I. (T.S.) _____

    1. _____

    2. _____

    3. _____

    4. _____

    5. _____

    6. _____

    7. _____

Clincher _____

Brainstorming for Ideas

Your goal is: to brainstorm for ideas with a parent or teacher

What are your general key words for a **topic sentence**?

What **strong verbs** will grab your reader's interest?

What **-ly words** will you add to your verbs? (See p. 13.)

What **quality adjectives** might describe these nouns? (See p. 9)
Arthur   legends   hero

What **who/which clause** will give your reader details? (See p. 25)

What **www.asia clause** might you put in the paragraph? (See p. 52)

What **-ly sentence openers** will add variety to your sentences? (See p. 91)

Composition Checklist

- ☐ name, date, left & right margins
- ☐ composition double-spaced
- ☐ title underlined (italicized if word processed)
- ☐ dress-ups underlined (one of each)
- ☐ sentence openers marked in margin
- ☐ no banned words

Clear topic sentence (key words highlighted)   _____

DRESS-UP (middle of sentence; underlined)	I
who/which clause	
-ly word	
strong verb	
quality adjective	
when, while, where, as, since, if, although	

OPENERS (first word of sentence; number in margin)	I
❸ -ly	

Clear clincher (repeats 2 or 3 highlighted words of T.S.)   _____

Title (repeats 2 or 3 words of clincher)   _____

For Parent/Teacher: Tips for Unit VII Creative Writing

❖ You have advanced this far. Bravo!

❖ Are you reading great literature aloud? Stretch their attentiveness, vocabulary and interests, imaginations and understanding of life.

❖ Refer to Appendix p. A-40 for links and ideas for additional literature.

❖ Maintain the discipline of outlining.

❖ A **key** to student success in this unit will be your planning ahead.

❖ Review for yourself *TWSS Syllabus/Seminar Workbook,* pp. 34–35, the Unit II key word outline model, the Unit III Story Sequence Chart, and the Unit III elements of a narrative story. Put the posters back up for all to see.

❖ Give lots of help as students outline and write a 1-paragraph fable and a 3-paragraph myth. Be able to explain what a **variation** and a **sequel** are.

❖ The new model in Unit VII is the Expanded Story Sequence Chart. Try to trust it. It works! Resist being legalistic about it. Make the new poster and put it up. If you still feel confused about the structure, sit down and write your own fairy tale. Then you'll get it!

❖ Three fairy tales have been contrived to help you and the children succeed with this 5-paragraph expanded story sequence model: "Little Red Hen," "A Christmas Carol," and "Rumpelstiltskin." "The Boy Who Cried Wolf" and Hans Christian Andersen's "The Little Mermaid" also work well.

❖ Follow the model. Enjoy asking the questions together and getting answers out of your brains—the way you did in Unit III. Paragraphs 2 and 3 further the plot as the character meets obstacles or seeks advice. The fourth paragraph continues the pattern, but toward the end, add more details so that you slow down the climax event.

❖ Allow students to choose what interests them. The process is more important than the product. Hands on structure and style; hands off content.

❖ Most importantly, as J. B. Webster exhorts in *Blended Structure & Style in Composition,* "Inspire your children with your enthusiasm and examples worthy of imitation. Creative writing cannot be taught; it must be caught."

Shoulder to the Wheel

Long ago a tired wagoner was driving a heavy load along a muddy road. At last he came to a part of the road where the wheels sank halfway into the mud. The more the horses pulled, the deeper the wheels sank. The wagoner knelt down and prayed that God would help him in his hour of need. Then he heard God say, "Get up, son, and put your shoulder to the wheel."

Moral: God helps those who help themselves.

God Says to Row

At the end of a long day, a fisherman was motoring his boat back to the dock. Suddenly, the motor stopped. He had run out of gas. The longer the fisherman tried to restart the motor, the farther he drifted back out to sea. The fisherman knelt down in the boat and prayed that God would send someone to tow him in. Then he thought he heard God chuckle and say, "Sit down, son, and row."

Moral: God helps those who help themselves.

Lesson 25a
The Variation

Your goals are: to recognize a variation
                     to take notes on the main ideas in the fable
                     to retell the fable from your key word outline

1. With a teacher or parent, read and talk about the two fables on p. 104. Did you notice that the main character's **problem** is basically the same in both of the fables? However, the **characters** differ. In the first fable he is a wagoner, but in the other he is a fisherman. The **setting** in the first fable is a wagon on a road. In the second fable, the setting is a boat at sea. Since the problem stays the same but the characters and setting change, the second fable is a *variation* of the first fable.

2. Review the process of creating a key word outline (p. 5). Then outline just **one** of the fables on p. 104. On each line below, write **2 or 3 words per each sentence**.

3. Get a partner and retell the fable—using only the outline—to each other.

Key Word Outline

I. _____

    1. _____

    2. _____

    3. _____

    4. _____

    5. _____

    6. _____

The Father and His Daughters

A man had two daughters, the older one married to a farmer, and the younger to a brick-maker. After a time, he went to the older daughter. She asked, "Father, please will you pray for a heavy fall of rain so that the crops may be well watered?" Not long after, he went to the younger daughter. She asked, "Father, please will you pray for the dry weather to continue so that the hot sunshine may dry the bricks?" He said to her, "If your sister asks for rain and you for dry weather, with which of you am I to join my prayers?"

Moral: You can't please everybody.

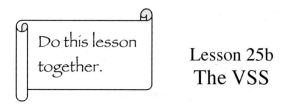
Do this lesson together.

Lesson 25b
The VSS

VSS stands for **very short sentence**. How short? 2–5 words. A vss is an attention grabber because it's so—short! For example, instead of writing

You probably won't be able to please everyone all the time,

the author of the fable wrote a vss: You can't please everybody.

When you write a vss in your paragraph, put a number **6** in the margin.

Your goals are: to take notes on the main ideas in the fable (p. 106)
to change the characters and the setting, with help
to write a **variation** of "The Father and His Daughters"

1. Take notes on the fable's main ideas by completing the outline below.
2. With a parent or teacher, brainstorm (p. 108).
3. Use this outline and page 108 to write a variation of "The Father and His Daughters." It should be a **1-paragraph fable with a moral**. Page 104 was a model that you can imitate. Use the composition checklist (p. 109).

Key Word Outline

I. _____

    1. _____

    2. _____

    3. _____

    4. _____

    5. _____

    6. _____

Brainstorming for Ideas

To write a variation, keep the **problem** but change the **characters** and the **setting**. The problem is that two characters want opposite things. What other kind of character could the father be? a grandparent? an animal? a teacher? What other kinds of characters could the daughters be? Where else could the story happen? under the sea? in a cave? in a jungle?

_____

What **strong verbs** will grab your reader's interest? Add **-ly words**. (p. 13)

_____

What **quality adjectives** might describe these nouns? (p. 9)
daughter   weather   prayers

_____

What **who/which clause** will give your reader details? (p. 25)

_____

What **www.asia clause** might you put in the fable? (p. 52)

_____

What **-ly sentence opener** will add variety to your sentences? (p. 91)

_____

Write a **vss** from one line of your key word outline. (p. 107)

Name_____

Composition Checklist

❏	name, date, left & right margins
❏	composition double-spaced
❏	title underlined (italicized if word processed)
❏	dress-ups underlined (one of each)
❏	sentence openers marked in margin
❏	no banned words

DRESS-UP (middle of sentence; underlined)	I
who/which clause	
-ly word	
strong verb	
quality adjective	
when, while, where, as, since, if, although	

OPENERS (first word of sentence when possible; number in margin)	I
❸ -ly	
❻ vss	

Final clincher (not the moral) _____

Title (repeats 2 or 3 words of clincher) _____

Perseus and Medusa

In ancient times, the Gorgon called Medusa lived on an island. She had snakes for hair, tusks like a boar, and sharp claws. Anyone who looked directly at a Gorgon turned to stone. Now the clever young Greek hero named Perseus had heard about this monster.

He decided he must kill Medusa. Fortunately, Perseus had the help of the gods on Mount Olympus. They gave him a sword to cut off Medusa's head and a bag to carry it in. Hermes, messenger of the gods, gave him winged sandals so that he could fly. Vulcan, the blacksmith god, created a helmet that made Perseus invisible. From Athena, he received a polished bronze shield. "Use it as a mirror," Athena instructed him. Perseus understood.

Flying backward, Perseus entered Medusa's lair, and he held his shield in front of his face. He could see the monster's face clearly, reflected in the shiny metal. Medusa herself was asleep, but the snakes on her head were not. They smelled someone nearby. With their poisonous fangs they jabbed at the air, but Perseus was invisible to them. Then the hero swung his sword, and the Gorgon's head fell—clunk—on the ground. Carefully he put it in the bag, because Medusa's face could still turn men into stone.

Hairspray*

The hero, Perseus, who was far from his home in Greece, continued to do brave deeds. Sometimes Medusa's head came in handy when he met someone who was mean to him. In the pouch, however, the snakes wriggled constantly. The blood dripped all over, too.

Perseus needed somewhere safe to put the head of the Gorgon. But where? On his winged sandals Perseus flew to the end of the earth. There the giant, Atlas, held up the heavens on his shoulders. Curious, he asked, "Perseus, may I peek at what's in that gross-looking bag?" Perseus turned his face away and pulled out the head. He knew what would happen. Fortunately, as Atlas was turning to stone, he whispered that Perseus must take Medusa's head to the wise goddess Athena.

So he did. Athena gladly received the, um, trophy. She placed it on a pedestal way up in the clouds, where it was safe. The other gods and goddesses thought Medusa's head was a great joke. They even named a movie after her—Hairspray.

*This myth is a **sequel** to p. 110. It keeps the characters and setting but the problem is different.

A Smart Hero*

Just yesterday the scary sound came out of a CD player in the family room. It was Earsplitter. This monster's sound was a mixture of a strange drumbeat, a loud guitar and bad words. Listening to it for more than two minutes turned people's brains into mashed potatoes. The smart hero Manuel had heard about the monster.

He decided to eject Earsplitter, but he needed help from friends. Mozart gave Manuel a beautiful melody. Then Bach gave him a civilized beat. Palestrina shared a gift of poetic words.

With his fingers in his ears and the weapons in his backpack, Manuel raced into the family room. He must act quickly, or in two minutes his brains would be mush. He ejected Earsplitter and put in Mozart's melody. Throwing the monster into the deepest, darkest dumpster, Manuel felt much smarter. Earsplitter would never mash brains again. From then on, Manuel was ready. When his dog would lie down under the ping pong table and put his paws over his ears, Manuel would run for his weapons. This smart hero vowed to help innocent listeners everywhere.

*This myth is a **variation** of p. 110. It keeps the problem but the characters and setting are different.

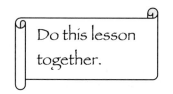

Do this lesson together.

Lesson 26
Write Your Own Myth

You have choices. You can write: 1) a sequel to "Perseus and Medusa" or a variation, 2) a sequel to "Odysseus and the Cyclops" (Appendix p. 35), or 3) a variation of "Jason and the Argonauts" (p. 36).

A variation keeps the problem but changes the characters and the setting. A sequel keeps the characters and the setting but changes the problem. Your myth will follow the Story Sequence Chart and will be 3 paragraphs long.

1. Review how to create an outline according to the Story Sequence Chart (p. 37). You can write your outline below, or on a separate sheet of paper if you need more room.

2. Brainstorm on page 114, and use the composition checklist on page 115.

Characters + Setting:

who?
like?
when?
where?

I. _____

  1. _____

  2. _____

  3. _____

Conflict:

what?
want or need?
think?
say?
do?

II. _____

  1. _____

  2. _____

  3. _____

  4. _____

Climax + Resolution:

how?
after?
learned?

Title repeats
final clincher

III. _____

  1. _____

  2. _____

  3. _____

  4. _____

Brainstorming for Ideas

Ask yourself questions about your **problem**, **characters** and **setting**. Write notes here:

_____

What **strong verbs** will grab your reader's interest? Add **-ly words**. (p. 13)

_____

What **who/which clauses** will give your reader details? (p. 25)

_____

What **www.asia clauses** might you put in the myth? (p. 52)

_____

What **-ly sentence openers** will add variety to your sentences? (p. 91)

_____

Write a **vss** *when possible*. (p. 107)

Name_____

Composition Checklist

☐	name, date, left & right margins
☐	composition double-spaced
☐	title underlined (italicized if word processed)
☐	Dress-ups are underlined (one of each).
☐	Sentence openers are marked in margin.
☐	no banned words

DRESS-UP (middle of sentence; underlined)	I	II	III
who/which clause			
-ly word			
strong verb			
quality adjective			
when, while, where, as, since, if, although			

OPENERS (first word of sentence when possible; number in margin)	I	II	III
❸ -ly			
❻ vss			

Final clincher   _____

Title (repeats 2 or 3 words of clincher)   _____

A Christmas Carol
Charles Dickens, 1834 (abridged)

It was Christmas Eve, long ago. The stingy, mean Ebenezer Scrooge had resented it when his clerk, Bob Cratchit, asked to spend Christmas Day with his family. "Christmas…. Humbug," Scrooge complained. Suddenly in his living room that night, he heard a noise. And then right through the locked door came the ghost of his business partner, Jacob Marley. He was dragging a heavy chain. How Jacob regretted the years when he had loved money but hated his fellow men. "You must learn to be kind while you still have a chance, Ebenezer. Three spirits will visit you. Expect the first when the bell chimes one."

Indeed, a strange figure did appear at one o'clock. The childlike spirit took Scrooge by the hand. "I am the Ghost of Christmas Past," it said. Together they traveled back in time to when Scrooge was a schoolboy, then an apprentice, and finally a young man. He had been engaged to a lovely girl named Belle. The spirit showed Scrooge the moment when she had told him goodbye. "You love gold more than anyone or anything, Ebenezer." Starting to feel sorry for his selfishness and greed, Scrooge begged the spirit to take him home.

Next, Scrooge woke to the sight of the merry Ghost of Christmas Present. In a second they were watching Christmas at the Cratchits' house. Bob Cratchit had just walked in with his youngest son, Tiny Tim, on his shoulder. Although Tim was sickly and crippled, he was full of Christmas joy. "God bless us, every one," he prayed at the dinner table. Being curious, Scrooge wondered if Tiny Tim would live, but the spirit, who could see the shadow of things to come, sadly shook his head. He also took Scrooge to see other destitute families.

Shocked, Scrooge realized that he should be helping them. Was his cold heart learning to love again?

Finally, there appeared the Ghost of Christmas Future, who was tall and covered over with a long black cloth. This spirit silently showed Scrooge the Cratchits' Christmas once again. It was hard for them to be joyful this time. Tiny Tim had died. Someone else had died, too, Scrooge noticed. The spirit had taken him to a graveyard. Could it be? There on a gravestone was his own name—Ebenezer Scrooge. "Spirit!" cried Ebenezer. "Hear me. I am not the man I was. I will not be uncaring any longer. I shall honor Christmas in my heart and try to keep it all the year. Taking care of my fellow men shall be my business from now on. Oh, tell me that I may change my fate!" Full of fear, Scrooge caught the spirit's hand. It faded away and became…a bedpost.

Yes! He was in his own room. Leaping out of bed, Scrooge danced around in little circles. He felt as happy as an angel! Then he ran and threw open the window. The people below were all wishing each other, "Happy Christmas!" He hadn't missed it. Scrooge sent a very surprised boy off to the market to buy a huge turkey for the Cratchit family. Then he gave Bob Cratchit a raise and lovingly took care of Tiny Tim. Most wonderful of all, Ebenezer Scrooge truly became a better person. It was always said of him that he kept Christmas well. May that be said of us, too. And so, as Tiny Tim would say, "God bless us, every one!

Lesson 27
Write Your Own Fairy Tale

For this writing experience, you have 2 choices. You can write your own version of either "A Christmas Carol" or "Rumpelstiltskin" (Appendix p. 36). Your fairy tale of 5 paragraphs will follow an expanded Story Sequence Chart:

I. _____
  1. _____
  2. _____
  3. _____
  4. _____
  5. _____

Background
Introduce characters + setting:
Who is in the story?
When does it happen?
Where do they live or go?
What is the problem?

What do they want or need?

II. _____
  1. _____
  2. _____
  3. _____
  4. _____
  5. _____

Character meets 1st obstacle or seeks advice 1st time.
What do they think? say? do?

Character meets 2nd obstacle or seeks advice 2nd time.
What do they think? say? do?

III. _____
  1. _____
  2. _____
  3. _____
  4. _____
  5. _____

Character meets 3rd obstacle or seeks advice 3rd time.
Slow down what they think, say and do + reach the climax.

How is the need resolved?

What happens after climax?
What is learned?
Is there a message?

Create an ending.
Title repeats final clincher.

❖ Read the tale together and discuss in terms of the expanded story sequence chart.

❖ Create an outline with words that show the story sequence.

❖ Brainstorm for dress-ups together.

❖ Use the checklist.

Brainstorming for Ideas

Ask yourself questions from the expanded Story Sequence Chart (p. 118).
Write notes here:

_____

What **strong verbs** will grab your reader's interest? Add **-ly words**. (p. 13)

_____

What **who/which clauses** will give your reader details? (p. 25)

_____

What **www.asia clauses** might you put in the fairy tale? (p. 52)

_____

What **-ly sentence openers** will add variety to your sentences? (p. 91)

_____

Write a **vss** *when possible*. (p. 107)

Name_____

Composition Checklist

- ☐ name, date, left & right margins
- ☐ composition double-spaced
- ☐ title underlined (italicized if word processed)
- ☐ dress-ups underlined (one of each)
- ☐ sentence openers marked in margin
- ☐ no banned words

DRESS-UP (middle of sentence; underlined)	I	II	III	IV	V
who/which clause					
-ly word					
strong verb					
quality adjective					
when, while, where, as, since, if, although					

OPENERS (first word of sentence; number in margin)	I	II	III	IV	V
❸ -ly					
❻ vss					

Final clincher _____

Title (repeats 2 or 3 words of clincher) _____

Little Red Hen
by
Greg

I. life, work, farm
   1. L.R. Hen, chicks
   2. Dog, Cat, lived, peace
   3. chore time, never helped
   4. planned, make bread
   5. needed, help

II. L.R. Hen, seeds, pail, field
   1. Dog, sleeping, road
   2. help, plant, seeds?
   3. not I, yawned, sleep

III. L.R. Hen, autumn, walked
   1. Cat, hunting
   2. help, harvest, wheat?
   3. not I, pounced, mouse

IV. L.R. Hen, bundle, mill
   1. miller, ground, flour
   2. kitchen, help, bake, bread?
   3. not I, do, myself
   4. delicious, help, eat?
   5. we will! Dog, Cat

V. anyone, helped, eat
   1. Dog, Cat, drooled
   2. L.R. Hen, fed, chicks
   3. best, bread, tasted
   4. L.R. Hen, clucked, smiled

For Little Red Hen and her chicks, who worked on an old farm, life was simple. ❸ Peacefully they lived together with Dog and Cat. Those two rarely helped when chore time came, however. Planning to make bread, Little Red Hen wished she could have some help.

With her pail which was full of seeds, Little Red Hen headed for the field. Dog was sleeping in the road just then. He woke up. ❻ She asked him if he would help plant the tiny seeds. "Not I," replied Dog. He yawned and immediately went back to sleep.

❸ Eventually, autumn came. Little Red Hen happily walked to the field. There she met Cat who was hunting mice. When asked to help harvest the wheat, since she was in the field, Cat refused. "Not I," she said. And she pounced on a fat mouse.

Little Red Hen eagerly bundled the wheat. Then she carried it to the mill where the miller ground it into fine flour. Bringing this back to her kitchen, Little Red Hen bumped into Dog and Cat again. Politely she asked for help while she baked the bread. Dog and Cat, who were a little lazy if you ask me, still replied, "Not I." Well, by this time Little Red Hen was used to doing all the work by herself, so she began to bake. In a jiffy, the breeze carried the delicious smell toward Dog and Cat. "Who will help me eat the bread?" called Little Red Hen. You guessed it, Dog and Cat volunteered.

❸ Justly, Little Red Hen announced that anyone could eat—who had helped. Then she fed her young chicks. Dog and cat drooled.❻ The chicks thought it was absolutely the best bread they had ever tasted. When she heard this, Little Red Hen clucked and smiled.

The Finale

Parents and teachers, however far into the units you have coached your students this year, surely they have written fables, myths or fairy tales that you and they can be proud of. Consider allowing them to present their literary achievements in front of each other, family and friends in The Finale. This program will be another ideal opportunity to build the children's self-confidence when speaking publicly and foster their audience's appreciation of great literature.

Their writings have been saved for just such an event. You needn't reinvent the wheel; perhaps try the same activities that worked for the Fable Festival (p. 32) or Mythical Masterpieces (p. 58). Review the objectives on page 3 as you're helping the students to speak from their key word outlines. Allow time for rehearsal(s) so they can polish their deliveries.

A few more ideas:

❖   If students have created artwork, display as much as possible. How could you group it? By student? By genre?

❖   By what simple means could the students compile their writings into individual anthologies? Even if only three-hole punched and placed in a folder, they would be able to show them, put them in the home or school library, and read them again.

❖   Do you know anyone who might be able to bind a large group of writings into a *Magnum Opus*? For example, all the children in a homeschooling family could publish writings from the year. An entire third grade class could do the same. What a marvelous achievement!

Appendix

Cinderella or The Little Glass Slipper
Charles Perrault

ONCE there was a gentleman who married, for his second wife, the proudest and most haughty woman that was ever seen. She had, by a former husband, two daughters of her own humor, who were, indeed, exactly like her in all things. He had likewise, by another wife, a young daughter, but of unparalleled goodness and sweetness of temper, which she took from her mother, who was the best creature in the world.

No sooner were the ceremonies of the wedding over but the mother-in-law began to show herself in her true colors. She could not bear the good qualities of this pretty girl, and the less because they made her own daughters appear the more odious. She employed her in the meanest work of the house: she scoured the dishes and tables, and scrubbed madam's chamber, and those of misses, her daughters; she lay up in a sorry garret, upon a wretched straw bed, while her sisters lay in fine rooms, with floors all inlaid, upon beds of the very newest fashion, and where they had looking-glasses so large that they might see themselves at their full length from head to foot.

The poor girl bore all patiently, and dared not tell her father, who would have rattled her off, for his wife governed him entirely. When she had done her work, she used to go into the chimney-corner, and sit down among cinders and ashes, which made her commonly be called Cinderwench; but the youngest, who was not so rude and uncivil as the eldest, called her Cinderella. However, Cinderella, notwithstanding her mean apparel, was a hundred times handsomer than her sisters, though they were always dressed very richly.

It happened that the King's son gave a ball, and invited all persons of fashion to it. Our young misses were also invited, for they cut a very grand figure among the quality. They were mightily delighted at this invitation, and wonderfully busy in choosing out such gowns, petticoats, and head-clothes as might become them. This was a new trouble to Cinderella; for it was she who ironed her sisters' linen, and plaited their ruffles; they talked all day long of nothing but how they should be dressed.

"For my part," said the eldest, "I will wear my red velvet suit with French trimming."

"And I," said the youngest, "shall have my usual petticoat; but then, to make amends for that, I will put on my gold-flowered manteau, and my diamond stomacher, which is far from being the most ordinary one in the world."

They sent for the best tire-woman they could get to make up their head-dresses and adjust their double pinners, and they had their red brushes and patches from Mademoiselle de la Poche.

Cinderella was likewise called up to them to be consulted in all these matters, for she had excellent notions, and advised them always for the best, nay, and offered her services to dress their heads, which they were very willing she should do. As she was doing this, they said to her:

"Cinderella, would you not be glad to go to the ball?"

"Alas!" said she, "you only jeer me; it is not for such as I am to go thither."

"Thou art in the right of it," replied they; " it would make the people laugh to see a Cinderwench at a ball."

Any one but Cinderella would have dressed their heads awry, but she was very good, and dressed them perfectly well. They were almost two days without eating, so much they were transported with joy. They broke above a dozen of laces in trying to be laced up close, that they might have a fine slender shape, and they were continually at their looking-glass. At last the happy day came; they went to Court, and Cinderella followed them with her eyes as long as she could, and when she had lost sight of them, she fell a-crying.

Her godmother, who saw her all in tears, asked her what was the matter.

"I wish I could—I wish I could…." She was not able to speak the rest, being interrupted by her tears and sobbing.

This godmother of hers, who was a fairy, said to her, "Thou wishest thou couldst go to the ball; is it not so?"

"Y—es," cried Cinderella, with a great sigh.

"Well," said her godmother, "be but a good girl, and I will contrive that thou shalt go." Then she took her into her chamber, and said to her, "Run into the garden, and bring me a pumpkin."

Cinderella went immediately to gather the finest she could get, and brought it to her godmother, not being able to imagine how this pumpkin could make her go to the ball. Her godmother scooped out all the inside of it, having left nothing but the rind; which done, she struck it with her wand, and the pumpkin was instantly turned into a fine coach, gilded all over with gold.

She then went to look into her mouse-trap, where she found six mice, all alive, and ordered Cinderella to lift up a little trapdoor, when, giving each mouse, as it went out, a little tap with her wand, the mouse was that moment turned into a fine horse, which altogether made a very fine set of six horses of a beautiful mouse-colored dapple-gray. Being at a loss for a coachman, "I will go and see," says Cinderella, " if there is a rat in the rat-trap—we may make a coachman of him."

"Thou art in the right," replied her godmother; "go and look."

Cinderella brought the trap to her, and in it there were three huge rats. The fairy made choice of one of the three which had the largest beard, and, having touched him with her wand, he was turned into a fat, jolly coachman, who had the smartest whiskers eyes ever beheld. After that, she said to her:

"Go again into the garden, and you will find six lizards behind the watering-pot, bring them to me."
She had no sooner done so but her godmother turned them into six footmen, who skipped up immediately behind the coach, with their liveries all bedaubed with gold and silver, and clung as close behind each other as if they had done nothing else their whole lives. The fairy then said to Cinderella:

"Well, you see here an equipage fit to go to the ball with; are you not pleased with it?"

"Oh! yes," cried she; "but must I go thither as I am, in these nasty rags?"

Her godmother only just touched her with her wand, and, at the same instant, her clothes were turned into cloth of gold and silver, all beset with jewels. This done, she gave her a pair of glass slippers, the prettiest in the whole world. Being thus decked out, she got up into her coach; but her godmother, above all things, commanded her not to stay till after midnight, telling her, at the same time, that if she stayed one moment longer, the coach would be a pumpkin again, her horses mice, her coachman a rat, her footmen lizards, and her clothes become just as they were before.

She promised her godmother she would not fail of leaving the ball before midnight; and then away she drives, scarce able to contain herself for joy. The King's son, who was told that a great princess, whom nobody knew, was come, ran out to receive her; he gave her his hand as she alighted out of the coach, and led her into the hall, among all the company. There was immediately a profound silence, they left off dancing, and the violins ceased to play, so attentive was every one to contemplate the singular beauties of the unknown new-comer. Nothing was then heard but a confused noise of:

"Ha! how handsome she is! Ha! how handsome she is!"

The King himself, old as he was, could not help watching her, and telling the Queen softly that it was a long time since he had seen so beautiful and lovely a creature.

All the ladies were busied in considering her clothes and headdress, that they might have some made next day after the same pattern, provided they could meet with such fine materials and as able hands to make them.

The King's son conducted her to the most honorable seat, and afterwards took her out to dance with him; she danced so very gracefully that they all more and more admired her. A fine collation was served up, whereof the young prince ate not a morsel, so intently was he busied in gazing on her.

She went and sat down by her sisters, showing them a thousand civilities, giving them part of the oranges and citrons which the Prince had presented her with, which very much surprised them, for they did not know her. While Cinderella was thus amusing her sisters, she heard the clock strike eleven and three-quarters, whereupon she immediately made a curtsy to the company and hasted away as fast as she could.

Being got home, she ran to seek out her godmother, and, after having thanked her, she said she could not but heartily wish she might go next day to the ball, because the King's son had desired her.

As she was eagerly telling her godmother whatever had passed at the ball, her two sisters knocked at the door, which Cinderella ran and opened.

"How long you have stayed!" cried she, gaping, rubbing her eyes and stretching herself as if she had been just waked out of her sleep; she had not, however, any manner of inclination to sleep since they went from home.

"If thou hadst been at the ball," says one of her sisters, "thou wouldst not have been tired with it. There came thither the finest princess, the most beautiful ever was seen with mortal eyes; she showed us a thousand civilities, and gave us oranges and citrons."

Cinderella seemed very indifferent in the matter; indeed, she asked them the name of that princess; but they told her they did not know it, and that the King's son was very uneasy on her account and would give all the world to know who she was. At this Cinderella, smiling, replied: "She must, then, be very beautiful indeed; how happy you have been! Could not I see her? Ah! dear Miss Charlotte, do lend me your yellow suit of clothes which you wear every day."

"Aye, to be sure!" cried Miss Charlotte; "Lend my clothes to such a dirty Cinderwench as thou art! I should be a fool."

Cinderella, indeed, expected well such answer, and was very glad of the refusal; for she would have been sadly put to it if her sister had lent her what she asked for jestingly.

The next day the two sisters were at the ball, and so was Cinderella, but dressed more magnificently than before. The King's son was always by her, and never ceased his compliments and kind speeches to her; to whom all this was so far from being tiresome that she quite forgot what her godmother had recommended to her; so that she, at last, counted the clock striking twelve when she took it to be no more than eleven; she then rose up and fled, as nimble as a deer. The Prince followed, but could not overtake her. She left behind one of her glass slippers, which the Prince took up most carefully. She got home, but quite out of breath, and in her nasty old clothes, having nothing left her of all her finery but one of the little slippers, fellow to that she dropped.

The guards at the palace gate were asked if they had not seen a princess go out. They said they had seen nobody go out but a young girl, very meanly dressed, and who had more the air of a poor country wench than a gentlewoman.

When the two sisters returned from the ball Cinderella asked them if they had been well diverted, and if the fine lady had been there. They told her yes, but that she hurried away immediately when it struck twelve, and with so much haste that she dropped one of her little glass slippers, the prettiest in the world, which the King's son had taken up; that he had done nothing but look at her all the time at the ball, and that most certainly he was very much in love with the beautiful person who owned the glass slipper.

What they said was very true; for a few days after, the King's son caused it to be proclaimed, by sound of trumpet, that he would marry her whose foot this slipper would just fit. They whom he employed began to try it upon the princesses, then the duchesses and all the Court, but in vain; it was brought to the two sisters, who did all they possibly could to thrust their foot into the slipper, but they could not effect it. Cinderella, who saw all this, and knew her slipper, said to them, laughing:

"Let me see if it will not fit me."

Her sisters burst out a-laughing, and began to banter her. The gentleman who was sent to try the slipper looked earnestly at Cinderella, and, finding her very handsome, said that it was but just that she should try, and that he had orders to let every one make trial.

He obliged Cinderella to sit down, and, putting the slipper to her foot, he found it went on very easily, and fitted her as if it had been made of wax. The astonishment her two sisters were in was excessively great, but still abundantly greater when Cinderella pulled out of her pocket the other slipper, and put it on her foot. Thereupon, in came her godmother, who, having touched with her wand Cinderella's clothes, made them richer and more magnificent than any of those she had before.

And now her two sisters found her to be that fine, beautiful lady whom they had seen at the ball. They threw themselves at her feet to beg pardon for all the ill-treatment they had made her undergo. Cinderella took them up, and, as she embraced them, cried that she forgave them with all her heart, and desired them always to love her.

She was conducted to the young Prince, dressed as she was; he thought her more charming than ever, and, a few days after, married her. Cinderella, who was no less good than beautiful, gave her two sisters lodgings in the palace, and that very same day matched them with two great lords of the Court.

———————————————

English Translation: Robert Samber (1729) in the Public Domain

BEAUTY AND THE BEAST

Jeanne-Marie LePrince de Beaumont

ONCE upon a time, in a very far-off country, there lived a merchant who had been so fortunate in all his undertakings that he was enormously rich. As he had, however, six sons and six daughters, he found that his money was not too much to let them all have everything they fancied, as they were accustomed to do.

But one day a most unexpected misfortune befell them. Their house caught fire and was speedily burnt to the ground, with all the splendid furniture, the books, pictures, gold, silver, and precious goods it contained; and this was only the beginning of their troubles. Their father, who had until this moment prospered in all ways, suddenly lost every ship he had upon the sea, either by dint of pirates, shipwreck, or fire. Then he heard that his clerks in distant countries, whom he trusted entirely, had proved unfaithful; and at last from great wealth he fell into the direst poverty.

All that he had left was a little house in a desolate place at least a hundred leagues from the town in which he had lived, and to this he was forced to retreat with his children, who were in despair at the idea of leading such a different life. Indeed, the daughters at first hoped that their friends, who had been so numerous while they were rich, would insist on their staying in their houses now they no longer possessed one. But they soon found that they were left alone, and that their former friends even attributed their misfortunes to their own extravagance, and showed no intention of offering them any help. So nothing was left for them but to take their departure to the cottage, which stood in the midst of a dark forest, and seemed to be the most dismal place upon the face of the earth. As they were too poor to have any servants, the girls had to work hard, like peasants, and the sons, for their part, cultivated the fields to earn their living. Roughly clothed, and living in the simplest way, the girls regretted unceasingly the luxuries and amusements of their former life; only the youngest tried to be brave and cheerful. She had been as sad as any one when misfortune first overtook her father, but, soon recovering her natural gaiety, she set to work to make the best of things, to amuse her father and brothers as well as she could, and to try to persuade her sisters to join her in dancing and singing. But they would do nothing of the sort, and, because she was not as doleful as themselves, they declared that this miserable life was all she was fit for. But she was really far prettier and cleverer than they were; indeed, she was so lovely that she was always called Beauty. After two years, when they were all beginning to get used to their new life, something happened to disturb their tranquility. Their father received the news that one of his ships, which he had believed to be lost, had come safely into port with a rich cargo. All the sons and daughters at once thought that their poverty was at an end, and wanted to set out directly for the town; but their father, who was more prudent, begged them to wait a little, and, though it was harvest-time, and he could ill be spared, determined to go himself first, to make inquires. Only the youngest daughter had any doubt but that they would soon again be as rich as they were before, or at least rich enough to live comfortably in some town where they would find amusement and gay companions once more. So they all loaded their father with commissions for jewels and dresses which it would have taken a fortune to buy; only Beauty, feeling sure that it was of no use, did not ask for anything. Her father, noticing her silence, said: "And what shall I bring for you, Beauty?"

"The only thing I wish for is to see you come home safely," she answered.

But this reply vexed her sisters, who fancied she was blaming them for having asked for such costly things. Her father, however, was pleased, but as he thought that at her age she certainly ought to like pretty presents, he told her to choose something.

"Well, dear father," she said, "as you insist upon it, I beg that you will bring me a rose. I have not seen one since we came here, and I love them so much."

So the merchant set out and reached the town as quickly as possible, but only to find that his former companions, believing him to be dead, had divided between them the goods which the ship had brought; and after six months of trouble and expense he found himself as poor as when he started, having been able to recover only just enough to pay the cost of his journey. To make matters worse, he was obliged to leave the town in the most terrible weather, so that by the time he was within a few leagues of his home he was almost exhausted with cold and fatigue. Though he knew it would take some hours to get through the forest, he was so anxious to be at his journey's end that he resolved to go on; but night overtook him, and the deep snow and bitter frost made it impossible for his horse to carry him any further. Not a house was to be seen; the only shelter he could get was the hollow trunk of a great tree, and there he crouched all the night, which seemed to him the longest he had ever known. In spite of his weariness the howling of the wolves kept him awake, and even when at last the day broke he was not much better off, for the falling snow had covered up every path, and he did not know which way to turn.

At length he made out some sort of track, and though at the beginning it was so rough and slippery that he fell down more than once, it presently became easier, and led him into an avenue of trees which ended in a splendid castle. It seemed to the merchant very strange that no snow had fallen in the avenue, which was entirely composed of orange trees, covered with flowers and fruit. When he reached the first court of the castle he saw before him a flight of agate steps, and went up them, and passed through several splendidly furnished rooms. The pleasant warmth of the air revived him, and he felt very hungry; but there seemed to be nobody in all this vast and splendid palace whom he could ask to give him something to eat. Deep silence reigned everywhere, and at last, tired of roaming through empty rooms and galleries, he stopped in a room smaller than the rest, where a clear fire was burning and a couch was drawn up cozily close to it. Thinking that this must be prepared for some one who was expected, he sat down to wait till he should come, and very soon fell into a sweet sleep.

When his extreme hunger wakened him after several hours, he was still alone; but a little table, upon which was a good dinner, had been drawn up close to him, and, as he had eaten nothing for twenty-four hours, he lost no time in beginning his meal, hoping that he might soon have an opportunity of thanking his considerate entertainer, whoever it might be. But no one appeared, and even after another long sleep, from which he awoke completely refreshed, there was no sign of anybody, though a fresh meal of dainty cakes and fruit was prepared upon the little table at his elbow. Being naturally timid, the silence began to terrify him, and he resolved to search once more through all the rooms; but it was of no use. Not even a servant was to be seen; there was no sign of life in the palace! He began to wonder what he should do, and to amuse himself by pretending that all the treasures he saw were his own, and considering how he would divide them among his children. Then he went down into the garden, and though it was winter everywhere else, here the sun shone, and the birds sang, and the flowers bloomed, and the air was soft and sweet. The merchant, in ecstasies with all he saw and heard, said to himself:

"All this must be meant for me. I will go this minute and bring my children to share all these delights."

In spite of being so cold and weary when he reached the castle, he had taken his horse to the stable and fed it. Now he thought he would saddle it for his homeward journey, and he turned down the path which led to the stable. This path had a hedge of roses on each side of it, and the merchant thought he had never seen or smelt such exquisite flowers. They reminded him of his promise to Beauty, and he stopped and had just gathered one to take to her when he was startled by a strange noise behind him. Turning round, he saw a frightful Beast, which seemed to be very angry and said, in a terrible voice:

"Who told you that you might gather my roses? Was it not enough that I allowed you to be in my palace and was kind to you? This is the way you show your gratitude, by stealing my flowers! But your insolence shall not go unpunished." The merchant, terrified by these furious words, dropped the fatal rose, and, throwing himself on his knees, cried: "Pardon me, noble sir. I am truly grateful to you for your hospitality, which was so magnificent that I could not imagine that you would be offended by my taking such a little thing as a rose." But the Beast's anger was not lessened by this speech.

"You are very ready with excuses and flattery," he cried; "but that will not save you from the death you deserve."

"Alas!" thought the merchant, "if my daughter Beauty could only know what danger her rose has brought me into!"

And in despair he began to tell the Beast all his misfortunes, and the reason of his journey, not forgetting to mention Beauty's request.

"A king's ransom would hardly have procured all that my other daughters asked," he said; "but I thought that I might at least take Beauty her rose. I beg you to forgive me, for you see I meant no harm."

The Beast considered for a moment, and then he said, in a less furious tone: "I will forgive you on one condition—that is, that you will give me one of your daughters."

"Ah!" cried the merchant, "if I were cruel enough to buy my own life at the expense of one of my children's, what excuse could I invent to bring her here?"

"No excuse would be necessary," answered the Beast. "If she comes at all she must come willingly. On no other condition will I have her. See if any one of them is courageous enough, and loves you well enough to come and save your life. You seem to be an honest man, so I will trust you to go home. I give you a month to see if either of your daughters will come back with you and stay here, to let you go free. If neither of them is willing, you must come alone, after bidding them good-by forever, for then you will belong to me. And do not imagine that you can hide from me, for if you fail to keep your word I will come and fetch you!" added the Beast grimly.

The merchant accepted this proposal, though he did not really think any of his daughters would be persuaded to come. He promised to return at the time appointed, and then, anxious to escape from the presence of the Beast, he asked permission to set off at once. But the Beast answered that he could not go until the next day.

"Then you will find a horse ready for you," he said. "Now go and eat your supper, and await my orders."

The poor merchant, more dead than alive, went back to his room where the most delicious supper was already served on the little table which was drawn up before a blazing fire. But he was too terrified to eat, and only tasted a few of the dishes, for fear the Beast should be angry if he did not obey his orders. When he had finished he heard a great noise in the next room, which he knew meant that the Beast was coming. As he could do nothing to escape his visit, the only thing that remained was to seem as little afraid as possible; so when the Beast appeared and asked roughly if he had supped well, the merchant answered humbly that he had, thanks to his host's kindness. Then the Beast warned him to remember their agreement, and to prepare his daughter exactly for what she had to expect.

"Do not get up to-morrow," he added, "until you see the sun and hear a golden bell ring. Then you will find your breakfast waiting for you here, and the horse you are to ride will be ready in the courtyard. He will also bring you back again when you come with your daughter a month hence. Farewell. Take a rose to Beauty, and remember your promise!"

The merchant was only too glad when the Beast went away, and though he could not sleep for sadness, he lay down until the sun rose. Then, after a hasty breakfast, he went to gather Beauty's rose, and mounted his horse, which carried him off so swiftly that in an instant he had lost sight of the palace, and he was still wrapped in gloomy thoughts when it stopped before the door of the cottage.

His sons and daughters, who had been very uneasy at his long absence, rushed to meet him, eager to know the result of his journey, which, seeing him mounted upon a splendid horse and wrapped in a rich mantle, they supposed to be favorable. But he hid the truth from them at first, only saying sadly to Beauty as he gave her the rose:

"Here is what you asked me to bring you; you little know what it has cost." But this excited their curiosity so greatly that presently he told them his adventures from beginning to end, and then they were all very unhappy. The girls lamented loudly over their lost hopes, and the sons declared that their father should not return to this terrible castle, and began to make plans for killing the Beast if it should come to fetch him. But he reminded them that he had promised to go back. Then the girls were very angry with Beauty, and said it was all her fault, and that if she had asked for something sensible this would never have happened, and complained bitterly that they should have to suffer for her folly.

Poor Beauty, much distressed, said to them: "I have indeed caused this misfortune, but I assure you I did it innocently. Who could have guessed that to ask for a rose in the middle of summer would cause so much misery? But as I did the mischief it is only just that I should suffer for it. I will therefore go back with my father to keep his promise."

At first nobody would hear of this arrangement, and her father and brothers, who loved her dearly, declared that nothing should make them let her go; but Beauty was firm. As the time drew near she divided all her little possessions between her sisters, and said good-by to everything she loved, and when the fatal day came she encouraged and cheered her father as they mounted together the horse which had brought him back. It seemed to fly rather than gallop, but so smoothly that Beauty was not frightened; indeed, she would have enjoyed the journey if she had not feared what might happen to her at the end of it. Her father still tried to persuade her to go back, but in vain. While they were talking the night fell, and then, to their great surprise, wonderful colored lights began to shine in all directions, and splendid fireworks blazed out before them; all the forest was illuminated by them, and even felt pleasantly warm, though it had been bitterly cold before. This lasted until they reached the avenue of orange trees, where were statues holding flaming torches, and when they got nearer to the palace they saw that it was illuminated from the roof to the ground, and music sounded softly from the courtyard. "The Beast must be very hungry," said Beauty, trying to laugh, "if he makes all this rejoicing over the arrival of his prey." But, in spite of her anxiety, she could not help admiring all the wonderful things she saw.

The horse stopped at the foot of the flight of steps leading to the terrace, and when they had dismounted her father led her to the little room he had been in before, where they found a splendid fire burning, and the table daintily spread with a delicious supper.

The merchant knew that this was meant for them, and Beauty, who was rather less frightened now that she had passed through so many rooms and seen nothing of the Beast, was quite willing to begin, for her long ride had made her very hungry. But they had hardly finished their meal when the noise of the Beast's footsteps was heard approaching, and Beauty clung to her father in terror, which became all the greater when she saw how frightened he was. But when the Beast really appeared, though she trembled at the sight of him, she made a great effort to hide her horror, and saluted him respectfully.

This evidently pleased the Beast. After looking at her he said, in a tone that might have struck terror into the boldest heart, though he did not seem to be angry:

"Good-evening, old man. Good-evening, Beauty."

The merchant was too terrified to reply, but Beauty answered sweetly:

"Good-evening, Beast."

"Have you come willingly?" asked the Beast. "Will you be content to stay here when your father goes away?"

Beauty answered bravely that she was quite prepared to stay.

"I am pleased with you," said the Beast. "As you have come of your own accord, you may stay. As for you, old man," he added, turning to the merchant, "at sunrise to-morrow you will take your departure. When the bell rings get up quickly and eat your breakfast, and you will find the same horse waiting to take you home; but remember that you must never expect to see my palace again."

Then turning to Beauty, he said: "Take your father into the next room, and help him to choose everything you think your brothers and sisters would like to have. You will find two traveling-trunks there; fill them as full as you can. It is only just that you should send them something very precious as a remembrance of yourself."

Then he went away, after saying, "Good-by, Beauty; good-by, old man;" and though Beauty was beginning to think with great dismay of her father's departure, she was afraid to disobey the Beast's orders; and they went into the next room, which had shelves and cupboards all round it. They were greatly surprised at the riches it contained. There were splendid dresses fit for a queen, with all the ornaments that were to be worn with them; and when Beauty opened the cupboards she was quite dazzled by the gorgeous jewels that lay in heaps upon every shelf. After choosing a vast quantity, which she divided between her sisters—for she had made a heap of the wonderful dresses for each of them— she opened the last chest, which was full of gold.

"I think, father," she said, "that, as the gold will be more useful to you, we had better take out the other things again, and fill the trunks with it." So they did this; but the more they put in, the more room there seemed to be, and at last they put back all the jewels and dresses they had taken out, and Beauty even added as many more of the jewels as she could carry at once; and then the trunks were not too full, but they were so heavy that an elephant could not have carried them!

"The Beast was mocking us," cried the merchant; "he must have pretended to give us all these things, knowing that I could not carry them away."

"Let us wait and see," answered Beauty. "I cannot believe that he meant to deceive us. All we can do it to fasten them up and leave them ready."
So they did this and returned to the little room, where, to their astonishment, they found breakfast ready. The merchant ate his with a good appetite, as the Beast's generosity made him believe that he might perhaps venture to come back soon and see Beauty. But she felt sure that her father was leaving her forever, so she was very sad when the bell rang sharply for the second time, and warned them that the time was come for them to part. They went down into the courtyard, where two horses were waiting, one loaded with the two trunks, the other for him to ride. They were pawing the ground in their impatience to start, and the merchant was forced to bid Beauty a hasty farewell; and as soon as he was mounted he went off at such a pace that she lost sight of him in an instant.

Then Beauty began to cry, and wandered sadly back to her own room. But she soon found that she was very sleepy, and as she had nothing better to do she lay down and instantly fell asleep. And then she dreamed that she was walking by a brook bordered with trees, and lamenting her sad fate, when a young prince, handsomer than any one she had ever seen, and with a voice that went straight to her heart, came and said to her, "Ah, Beauty! You are not so unfortunate as you suppose. Here you will be rewarded for all you have suffered elsewhere. Your every wish shall be gratified. Only try to find me out, no matter how I may be disguised, as I love you dearly, and in making me happy you will find your own happiness. Be as true-hearted as you are beautiful, and we shall have nothing left to wish for."

"What can I do, Prince, to make you happy?" said Beauty.

"Only be grateful," he answered, "and do not trust too much to your eyes. And, above all, do not desert me until you have saved me from my cruel misery." After this she thought she found herself in a room with a stately and beautiful lady, who said to her:

"Dear Beauty, try not to regret all you have left behind you, for you are destined to a better fate. Only do not let yourself be deceived by appearances."

Beauty found her dreams so interesting that she was in no hurry to awake, but presently the clock roused her by calling her name softly twelve times, and then she got up and found her dressing-table set out with everything she could possibly want; and when her toilet was finished she found dinner was waiting in the room next to hers. But dinner does not take very long when you are all by yourself, and very soon she sat down cozily in the corner of a sofa, and began to think about the charming Prince she had seen in her dream.

"He said I could make him happy," said Beauty to herself.

"It seems, then, that this horrible Beast keeps him a prisoner. How can I set him free? I wonder why they both told me not to trust to appearances? I don't understand it. But, after all, it was only a dream, so why should I trouble myself about it? I had better go and find something to do to amuse myself."

So she got up and began to explore some of the many rooms of the palace. The first she entered was lined with mirrors, and Beauty saw herself reflected on every side, and thought she had never seen such a charming room. Then a bracelet which was hanging from a chandelier caught her eye, and on taking it down she was greatly surprised to find that it held a portrait of her unknown admirer, just as she had seen him in her dream. With great delight she slipped the bracelet on her arm, and went on into a gallery of pictures, where she soon found a portrait of the same handsome Prince, as large as life, and so well painted that as she studied it he seemed to smile kindly at her. Tearing herself away from the portrait at last, she passed through into a room which contained every musical instrument under the sun, and here she amused herself for a long while in trying some of them, and singing until she was tired. The next room was a library, and she saw everything she had ever wanted to read, as well as everything she had read, and it seemed to her that a whole lifetime would not be enough even to read the names of the books, there were so many. By this time it was growing dusk, and wax candles in diamond and ruby candlesticks were beginning to light themselves in every room.

Beauty found her supper served just at the time she preferred to have it, but she did not see any one or hear a sound, and, though her father had warned her that she would be alone, she began to find it rather dull.

But presently she heard the Beast coming, and wondered tremblingly if he meant to eat her up now.

However, as he did not seem at all ferocious, and only said gruffly:

"Good-evening, Beauty." She answered cheerfully and managed to conceal her terror. Then the Beast asked her how she had been amusing herself, and she told him all the rooms she had seen.

Then he asked if she thought she could be happy in his palace; and Beauty answered that everything was so beautiful that she would be very hard to please if she could not be happy. And after about an hour's talk Beauty began to think that the Beast was not nearly so terrible as she had supposed at first. Then he got up to leave her, and said in his gruff voice:

"Do you love me, Beauty? Will you marry me?"

"Oh! what shall I say?" cried Beauty, for she was afraid to make the Beast angry by refusing.

"Say 'yes' or 'no' without fear," he replied.

"Oh! no, Beast," said Beauty hastily.

"Since you will not, good-night, Beauty," he said.

And she answered: "Good-night, Beast," very glad to find that her refusal had not provoked him. And after he was gone she was very soon in bed and asleep, and dreaming of her unknown Prince. She thought he came and said to her: "Ah, Beauty! why are you so unkind to me? I fear I am fated to be unhappy for many a long day still." And then her dreams changed, but the charming Prince figured in them all; and when morning came her first thought was to look at the portrait and see if it was really like him, and she found that it certainly was.

This morning she decided to amuse herself in the garden, for the sun shone, and all the fountains were playing; but she was astonished to find that every place was familiar to her, and presently she came to the brook where the myrtle trees were growing where she had first met the Prince in her dream, and that made her think more than ever that he must be kept a prisoner by the Beast. When she was tired she went back to the palace, and found a new room full of materials for every kind of work—ribbons to make into bows, and silks to work into flowers. Then there was an aviary full of rare birds, which were so tame that they flew to Beauty as soon as they saw her, and perched upon her shoulders and her head.

"Pretty little creatures," she said, "how I wish that your cage was nearer to my room, that I might often hear you sing!"

So saying she opened a door, and found to her delight that it led into her own room, though she had thought it was quite the other side of the palace. There were more birds in a room farther on, parrots and cockatoos that could talk, and they greeted Beauty by name; indeed, she found them so entertaining that she took one or two back to her room, and they talked to her while she was at supper; after which the Beast paid her his usual visit, and asked the same question as before, and then with a gruff "good-night" he took his departure, and Beauty went to bed to dream of her mysterious Prince. The days passed swiftly in different amusements, and after a while Beauty found out another strange thing in the palace, which often pleased her when she was tired of being alone. There was one room which she had not noticed particularly; it was empty, except that under each of the windows stood a very comfortable chair; and the first time she had looked out of the window it had seemed to her that a black curtain prevented her from seeing anything outside. But the second time she went into the room, happening to be tired, she sat down in one of the chairs, when instantly the curtain was rolled aside, and a most amusing pantomime was acted before her; there were dances, and colored lights, and music, and pretty dresses, and it was all so gay that Beauty was in ecstasies. After that she tried the other seven windows in turn, and there was some new surprising entertainment to be seen from each of them, so that Beauty never could feel lonely any more. Every evening after supper the Beast came to see her, and always before saying good-night asked her in his terrible voice:

"Beauty, will you marry me?"

And it seemed to Beauty, now she understood him better, that when she said, "No, Beast," he went away quite sad. But her happy dreams of the handsome young Prince soon made her forget the poor Beast, and the only thing that at all disturbed her was to be constantly told to distrust appearances, to let her heart guide her, and not her eyes, and many other equally perplexing things, which, consider as she would, she could not understand.

So everything went on for a long time, until at last, happy as she was, Beauty began to long for the sight of her father and her brothers and sisters; and one night, seeing her look very sad, the Beast asked her what was the matter. Beauty had quite ceased to be afraid of him. Now she knew that he was really gentle in spite of his ferocious looks and his dreadful voice. So she answered that she was longing to see her home once more. Upon hearing this the Beast seemed sadly distressed, and cried miserably.

"Ah! Beauty, have you the heart to desert an unhappy Beast like this? What more do you want to make you happy? Is it because you hate me that you want to escape?"

"No, dear Beast," answered Beauty softly, "I do not hate you, and I should be very sorry never to see you any more, but I long to see my father again. Only let me go for two months, and I promise to come back to you and stay for the rest of my life."

The Beast, who had been sighing dolefully while she spoke, now replied: "I cannot refuse you anything you ask, even though it should cost me my life. Take the four boxes you will find in the room next to your own, and fill them with everything you wish to take with you. But remember your promise and come back when the two months are over, or you may have cause to repent it, for if you do not come in good time you will find your faithful Beast dead. You will not need any chariot to bring you back. Only say good-by to all your brothers and sisters the night before you come away, and when you have gone to bed turn this ring round upon your finger and say firmly: 'I wish to go back to my palace and see my Beast again.' Good-night, Beauty. Fear nothing, sleep peacefully, and before long you shall see your father once more."

As soon as Beauty was alone she hastened to fill the boxes with all the rare and precious things she saw about her, and only when she was tired of heaping things into them did they seem to be full.

Then she went to bed, but could hardly sleep for joy. And when at last she did begin to dream of her beloved Prince she was grieved to see him stretched upon a grassy bank sad and weary, and hardly like himself.

"What is the matter?" she cried.

But he looked at her reproachfully, and said: "How can you ask me, cruel one? Are you not leaving me to my death perhaps?"

"Ah! don't be so sorrowful," cried Beauty; "I am, only going to assure my father that I am safe and happy. I have promised the Beast faithfully that I will come back, and he would die of grief if I did not keep my word!"

"What would that matter to you?" said the Prince. "Surely you would not care?"

"Indeed I should be ungrateful if I did not care for such a kind Beast," cried Beauty indignantly. "I would die to save him from pain. I assure you it is not his fault that he is so ugly."

Just then a strange sound woke her—some one was speaking not very far away; and opening her eyes she found herself in a room she had never seen before, which was certainly not nearly so splendid as those she was used to in the Beast's palace. Where could she be? She got up and dressed hastily, and then saw that the boxes she had packed the night before were all in the room. While she was wondering by what magic the Beast had transported them and herself to this strange place she suddenly heard her father's voice, and rushed out and greeted him joyfully. Her brothers and sisters were all astonished at her appearance, as they had never expected to see her again, and there was no end to the questions they asked her. She had also much to hear about what had happened to them while she was away, and of her father's journey home. But when they heard that she had only come to be with them for a short time, and then must go back to the Beast's palace forever, they lamented loudly. Then

Beauty asked her father what he thought could be the meaning of her strange dreams, and why the Prince constantly begged her not to trust to appearances. After much consideration he answered: "You tell me yourself that the Beast, frightful as he is, loves you dearly, and deserves your love and gratitude for his gentleness and kindness; I think the Prince must mean you to understand that you ought to reward him by doing as he wishes you to, in spite of his ugliness."

Beauty could not help seeing that this seemed very probable; still, when she thought of her dear Prince who was so handsome, she did not feel at all inclined to marry the Beast. At any rate, for two months she need not decide, but could enjoy herself with her sisters. But though they were rich now, and lived in a town again, and had plenty of acquaintances, Beauty found that nothing amused her very much; and she often thought of the palace, where she was so happy, especially as at home she never once dreamed of her dear Prince, and she felt quite sad without him.

Then her sisters seemed to have got quite used to being without her, and even found her rather in the way, so she would not have been sorry when the two months were over but for her father and brothers, who begged her to stay, and seemed so grieved at the thought of her departure that she had not the courage to say good-by to them. Every day when she got up she meant to say it at night, and when night came she put it off again, until at last she had a dismal dream which helped her to make up her mind. She thought she was wandering in a lonely path in the palace gardens when she heard groans which seemed to come from some bushes hiding the entrance of a cave, and running quickly to see what could be the matter, she found the Beast stretched out upon his side, apparently dying. He reproached her faintly with being the cause of his distress, and at the same moment a stately lady appeared, and said very gravely:

"Ah! Beauty, you are only just in time to save his life. See what happens when people do not keep their promises! If you had delayed one day more, you would have found him dead."

Beauty was so terrified by this dream that the next morning she announced her intention of going back at once, and that very night she said good-by to her father and all her brothers and sisters, and as soon as she was in bed she turned her ring round upon her finger, and said firmly:

"I wish to go back to my palace and see my Beast again," as she had been told to do.

Then she fell asleep instantly, and only woke up to hear the clock saying, "Beauty, Beauty," twelve times in its musical voice, which told her at once that she was really in the palace once more. Everything was just as before, and her birds were so glad to see her! But Beauty thought she had never known such a long day, for she was so anxious to see the Beast again that, she felt as if supper-time would never come.

But when it did come and no Beast appeared she was really frightened; so, after listening and waiting for a long time, she ran down into the garden to search for him. Up and down the paths and avenues ran poor Beauty, calling him in vain, for no one answered, and not a trace of him could she find; until at last, quite tired, she stopped for a minute's rest, and saw that she was standing opposite the shady path she had seen in her dream. She rushed down it, and, sure enough, there was the cave, and in it lay the Beast—asleep, as Beauty thought. Quite glad to have found him, she ran up and stroked his head, but to her horror he did not move or open his eyes.

"Oh! he is dead; and it is all my fault," said Beauty, crying bitterly.

But then, looking at him again, she fancied he still breathed and, hastily fetching some water from the nearest fountain, she sprinkled it over his face, and to her great delight he began to revive.

"Oh! Beast, how you frightened me!" she cried. "I never knew how much I loved you until just now, when I feared I was too late to save your life."

"Can you really love such an ugly creature as I am?" said the Beast faintly. "Ah! Beauty, you only came just in time. I was dying because I thought you had forgotten your promise. But go back now and rest, I shall see you again by-and-by."

Beauty, who had half expected that he would be angry with her, was reassured by his gentle voice, and went back to the palace, where supper was awaiting her; and afterwards the Beast came in as usual, and talked about the time she had spent with her father, asking if she had enjoyed herself, and if they had all been very glad to see her.

Beauty answered politely, and quite enjoyed telling him all that had happened to her. And when at last the time came for him to go, and he asked, as he had so often asked before:

"Beauty, will you marry me?"

She answered softly: "Yes, dear Beast."

As she spoke a blaze of light sprang up before the windows of the palace; fireworks crackled and guns banged, and across the avenue of orange trees, in letters all made of fire-flies, was written: "Long live the Prince and his Bride." Turning to ask the Beast what it could all mean, Beauty found that he had disappeared, and in his place stood her long-loved Prince! At the same moment the wheels of a chariot were heard upon the terrace, and two ladies entered the room. One of them Beauty recognized as the stately lady she had seen in her dreams; the other was also so grand and queenly that Beauty hardly knew which to greet first.

But the one she already knew said to her companion:

"Well, Queen, this is Beauty, who has had the courage to rescue your son from the terrible enchantment. They love one another, and only your consent to their marriage is wanting to make them perfectly happy."

"I consent with all my heart," cried the Queen.

"How can I ever thank you enough, charming girl, for having restored my dear son to his natural form?" And then she tenderly embraced Beauty and the Prince, who had meanwhile been greeting the Fairy and receiving her congratulations.

"Now," said the Fairy to Beauty, "I suppose you would like me to send for all your brothers and sisters to dance at your wedding?"

And so she did, and the marriage was celebrated the very next day with the utmost splendor, and Beauty and the Prince lived happily ever after.

The Ugly Duckling

Hans Christian Andersen

It was lovely summer weather in the country, and the golden corn, the green oats, and the haystacks piled up in the meadows looked beautiful. The stork walking about on his long red legs chattered in the Egyptian language, which he had learnt from his mother. The corn-fields and meadows were surrounded by large forests, in the midst of which were deep pools. It was, indeed, delightful to walk about in the country. In a sunny spot stood a pleasant old farm-house close by a deep river, and from the house down to the waterside grew great burdock leaves, so high, that under the tallest of them a little child could stand upright. The spot was as wild as the centre of a thick wood. In this snug retreat sat a duck on her nest, watching for her young brood to hatch; she was beginning to get tired of her task, for the little ones were a long time coming out of their shells, and she seldom had any visitors. The other ducks liked much better to swim about in the river than to climb the slippery banks, and sit under a burdock leaf, to have a gossip with her. At length one shell cracked, and then another, and from each egg came a living creature that lifted its head and cried, "Peep, peep." "Quack, quack," said the mother, and then they all quacked as well as they could, and looked about them on every side at the large green leaves. Their mother allowed them to look as much as they liked, because green is good for the eyes. "How large the world is," said the young ducks, when they found how much more room they now had than while they were inside the egg-shell. "Do you imagine this is the whole world?" asked the mother. "Wait till you have seen the garden; it stretches far beyond that to the parson's field, but I have never ventured to such a distance. Are you all out?" she continued, rising. "No, I declare, the largest egg lies there still. I wonder how long this is to last, I am quite tired of it." And she seated herself again on the nest.

"Well, how are you getting on?" asked an old duck, who paid her a visit.

"One egg is not hatched yet," said the duck. "It will not break. But just look at all the others; are they not the prettiest little ducklings you ever saw? They are the image of their father, who is so unkind, he never comes to see."

"Let me see the egg that will not break," said the duck. "I have no doubt it is a turkey's egg. I was persuaded to hatch some once, and after all my care and trouble with the young ones, they were afraid of the water. I quacked and clucked, but all to no purpose. I could not get them to venture in. Let me look at the egg. Yes, that is a turkey's egg; take my advice, leave it where it is and teach the other children to swim."

"I think I will sit on it a little while longer," said the duck. "As I have sat so long already, a few days will be nothing."

"Please yourself," said the old duck, and she went away.

At last the large egg broke, and a young one crept forth crying, "Peep, peep." It was very large and ugly. The duck stared at it and exclaimed, "It is very large and not at all like the others. I wonder if it really is a turkey. We shall soon find it out, however when we go to the water. It must go in, if I have to push it myself."

On the next day the weather was delightful, and the sun shone brightly on the green burdock leaves, so the mother duck took her young brood down to the water, and jumped in with a splash. "Quack, quack," cried she, and one after another the little ducklings jumped in. The water closed over their heads, but they came up again in an instant, and swam about quite prettily with their legs paddling under them as easily as possible, and the ugly duckling was also in the water swimming with them.

"Oh," said the mother, "that is not a turkey; how well he uses his legs, and how upright he holds himself! He is my own child, and he is not so very ugly after all if you look at him properly. Quack, quack! Come with me now, I will take you into grand society, and introduce you to the farmyard, but you must keep close to me or you may be trodden upon; and, above all, beware of the cat."

When they reached the farmyard, there was a great disturbance; two families were fighting for an eel's head, which, after all, was carried off by the cat. "See, children, that is the way of the world," said the mother duck, whetting her beak, for she would have liked the eel's head herself. "Come, now, use your legs, and let me see how well you can behave. You must bow your heads prettily to that old duck yonder. She is the highest born of them all, and has Spanish blood, therefore, she is well off. Don't you see she has a red flag tied to her leg, which is something very grand, and a great honor for a duck; it shows that every one is anxious not to lose her, as she can be recognized both by man and beast. Come, now, don't turn your toes, a well-bred duckling spreads his feet wide apart, just like his father and mother, in this way; now bend your neck, and say 'quack.'"

The ducklings did as they were bid, but the other duck stared, and said, "Look, here comes another brood, as if there were not enough of us already! And what a queer looking object one of them is; we don't want him here." And then one flew out and bit him in the neck.

"Let him alone," said the mother. "He is not doing any harm."

"Yes, but he is so big and ugly," said the spiteful duck, "and therefore he must be turned out."

"The others are very pretty children," said the old duck, with the rag on her leg, "all but that one; I wish his mother could improve him a little."

"That is impossible, your grace," replied the mother. "He is not pretty, but he has a very good disposition, and swims as well or even better than the others. I think he will grow up pretty, and perhaps be smaller; he has remained too long in the egg, and therefore his figure is not properly formed." And then she stroked his neck and smoothed the feathers, saying, "It is a drake, and therefore not of so much consequence. I think he will grow up strong, and able to take care of himself."

"The other ducklings are graceful enough," said the old duck. "Now make yourself at home, and if you can find an eel's head, you can bring it to me."

And so they made themselves comfortable; but the poor duckling, who had crept out of his shell last of all, and looked so ugly, was bitten and pushed and made fun of, not only by the ducks, but by all the poultry. "He is too big," they all said, and the turkey cock, who had been born into the world with spurs, and fancied himself really an emperor, puffed himself out like a vessel in full sail, and flew at the duckling, and became quite red in the head with passion, so that the poor little thing did not know where to go, and was quite miserable because he was so ugly and laughed at by the whole farmyard. So it went on from day to day till it got worse and worse. The poor duckling was driven about by every one; even his brothers and sisters were unkind to him, and would say, "Ah, you ugly creature, I wish the cat would get you," and his mother said she wished he had never been born. The ducks pecked him, the chickens beat him, and the girl who fed the poultry kicked him with her feet. So at last he ran away, frightening the little birds in the hedge as he flew over the palings.

"They are afraid of me because I am ugly," he said. So he closed his eyes, and flew still farther, until he came out on a large moor, inhabited by wild ducks. Here he remained the whole night, feeling very tired and sorrowful.

In the morning, when the wild ducks rose in the air, they stared at their new comrade. "What sort of a duck are you?" they all said, coming round him.

He bowed to them, and was as polite as he could be, but he did not reply to their question. "You are exceedingly ugly," said the wild ducks, "but that will not matter if you do not want to marry one of our family."

Poor thing! He had no thoughts of marriage; all he wanted was permission to lie among the rushes, and drink some of the water on the moor. After he had been on the moor two days, there came two wild geese, or rather goslings, for they had not been out of the egg long, and were very saucy. "Listen, friend," said one of them to the duckling, "you are so ugly, that we like you very well. Will you go with us, and become a bird of passage? Not far from here is another moor, in which there are some pretty wild geese, all unmarried. It is a chance for you to get a wife; you may be lucky, ugly as you are."

"Pop, pop," sounded in the air, and the two wild geese fell dead among the rushes, and the water was tinged with blood. "Pop, pop," echoed far and wide in the distance, and whole flocks of wild geese rose up from the rushes. The sound continued from every direction, for the sportsmen surrounded the moor, and some were even seated on branches of trees, overlooking the rushes. The blue smoke from the guns rose like clouds over the dark trees, and as it floated away across the water, a number of sporting dogs bounded in among the rushes, which bent beneath them wherever they went. How they terrified the poor duckling! He turned away his head to hide it under his wing, and at the same moment a large terrible dog passed quite near him. His jaws were open, his tongue hung from his mouth, and his eyes glared fearfully. He thrust his nose close to the duckling, showing his sharp teeth, and then, "splash, splash," he went into the water without touching him. "Oh," sighed the duckling, "how thankful I am for being so ugly; even a dog will not bite me." And so he lay quite still, while the shot rattled through the rushes, and gun after gun was fired over him. It was late in the day before all became quiet, but even then the poor young thing did not dare to move. He waited quietly for several hours, and then, after looking carefully around him, hastened away from the moor as fast as he could. He ran over field and meadow till a storm arose, and he could hardly struggle against it. Towards evening, he reached a poor little cottage that seemed ready to fall, and only remained standing because it could not decide on which side to fall first. The storm continued so violent, that the duckling could go no farther; he sat down by the cottage, and then he noticed that the door was not quite closed in consequence of one of the hinges having given way. There was therefore a narrow opening near the bottom large enough for him to slip through, which he did very quietly, and got a shelter for the night. A woman, a tom cat, and a hen lived in this cottage. The tom cat, whom the mistress called, "My little son", was a great favorite; he could raise his back, and purr, and could even throw out sparks from his fur if it were stroked the wrong way. The hen had very short legs, so she was called "Chickie short legs". She laid good eggs, and her mistress loved her as if she had been her own child. In the morning, the strange visitor was discovered, and the tom cat began to purr, and the hen to cluck.

"What is that noise about?" said the old woman, looking round the room, but her sight was not very good; therefore, when she saw the duckling she thought it must be a fat duck that had strayed from home. "Oh what a prize!" she exclaimed. "I hope it is not a drake, for then I shall have some duck's eggs. I must wait and see." So the duckling was allowed to remain on trial for three weeks, but there were no eggs. Now the tom cat was the master of the house, and the hen was mistress, and they always said, "We and the world," for they believed themselves to be half the world, and the better half too. The duckling thought that others might hold a different opinion on the subject, but the hen would not listen to such doubts. "Can you lay eggs?" she asked. "No." "Then have the goodness to hold your tongue." "Can you raise your back, or purr, or throw out sparks?" said the tom cat. "No." "Then you have no right to express an opinion when sensible people are speaking." So the duckling sat in a corner, feeling very low spirited, till the sunshine and the fresh air came into the room through the open door, and then he began to feel such a great longing for a swim on the water, that he could not help telling the hen.

"What an absurd idea," said the hen. "You have nothing else to do, therefore you have foolish fancies. If you could purr or lay eggs, they would pass away."

"But it is so delightful to swim about on the water," said the duckling, "and so refreshing to feel it close over your head, while you dive down to the bottom."

A-28

"Delightful, indeed!" said the hen, "Why you must be crazy! Ask the cat, he is the cleverest animal I know. Ask him how he would like to swim about on the water, or to dive under it, for I will not speak of my own opinion. Ask our mistress, the old woman. There is no one in the world more clever than she is. Do you think she would like to swim, or to let the water close over her head?"

"You don't understand me," said the duckling.

"We don't understand you? Who can understand you, I wonder? Do you consider yourself more clever than the cat, or the old woman? I will say nothing of myself. Don't imagine such nonsense, child, and thank your good fortune that you have been received here. Are you not in a warm room, and in society from which you may learn something? But you are a chatterer, and your company is not very agreeable. Believe me, I speak only for your own good. I may tell you unpleasant truths, but that is a proof of my friendship. I advise you, therefore, to lay eggs, and learn to purr as quickly as possible."

"I believe I must go out into the world again," said the duckling.

"Yes, do," said the hen. So the duckling left the cottage, and soon found water on which it could swim and dive, but was avoided by all other animals, because of its ugly appearance. Autumn came, and the leaves in the forest turned to orange and gold. Then, as winter approached, the wind caught them as they fell and whirled them in the cold air. The clouds, heavy with hail and snow-flakes, hung low in the sky, and the raven stood on the ferns crying, "Croak, croak." It made one shiver with cold to look at him. All this was very sad for the poor little duckling. One evening, just as the sun set amid radiant clouds, there came a large flock of beautiful birds out of the bushes. The duckling had never seen any like them before. They were swans, and they curved their graceful necks, while their soft plumage shown with dazzling whiteness. They uttered a singular cry, as they spread their glorious wings and flew away from those cold regions to warmer countries across the sea. As they mounted higher and higher in the air, the ugly little duckling felt quite a strange sensation as he watched them. He whirled himself in the water like a wheel, stretched out his neck towards them, and uttered a cry so strange that it frightened himself. Could he ever forget those beautiful, happy birds? And when at last they were out of his sight, he dived under the water, and rose again almost beside himself with excitement. He knew not the names of these birds, nor where they had flown, but he felt towards them as he had never felt for any other bird in the world. He was not envious of these beautiful creatures, but wished to be as lovely as they. Poor ugly creature, how gladly he would have lived even with the ducks had they only given him encouragement. The winter grew colder and colder; he was obliged to swim about on the water to keep it from freezing, but every night the space on which he swam became smaller and smaller. At length it froze so hard that the ice in the water crackled as he moved, and the duckling had to paddle with his legs as well as he could, to keep the space from closing up. He became exhausted at last, and lay still and helpless, frozen fast in the ice.

Early in the morning, a peasant, who was passing by, saw what had happened. He broke the ice in pieces with his wooden shoe, and carried the duckling home to his wife. The warmth revived the poor little creature; but when the children wanted to play with him, the duckling thought they would do him some harm; so he started up in terror, fluttered into the milk-pan, and splashed the milk about the room. Then the woman clapped her hands, which frightened him still more. He flew first into the butter-cask, then into the meal-tub, and out again. What a condition he was in! The woman screamed, and struck at him with the tongs; the children laughed and screamed, and tumbled over each other, in their efforts to catch him, but luckily he escaped. The door stood open; the poor creature could just manage to slip out among the bushes, and lie down quite exhausted in the newly fallen snow.

It would be very sad, were I to relate all the misery and privations which the poor little duckling endured during the hard winter; but when it had passed, he found himself lying one morning in a moor, amongst the rushes. He felt the warm sun shining, and heard the lark singing, and saw that all around was beautiful spring. Then the young bird felt that his wings were strong, as he flapped them against his sides, and rose high into the air. They bore him onwards, until he found himself in a large garden, before he well knew how it had happened. The apple-trees were in full blossom, and the fragrant elders bent their long green branches down to the stream which wound round a smooth lawn. Everything looked beautiful, in the freshness of early spring. From a thicket close by came three beautiful white swans, rustling their feathers, and swimming lightly over the smooth water. The duckling remembered the lovely birds, and felt more strangely unhappy than ever.

"I will fly to those royal birds," he exclaimed, "and they will kill me, because I am so ugly, and dare to approach them; but it does not matter. Better be killed by them than pecked by the ducks, beaten by the hens, pushed about by the maiden who feeds the poultry, or starved with hunger in the winter."

Then he flew to the water, and swam towards the beautiful swans. The moment they espied the stranger, they rushed to meet him with outstretched wings.

"Kill me," said the poor bird; and he bent his head down to the surface of the water, and awaited death.

But what did he see in the clear stream below? His own image, no longer a dark, gray bird, ugly and disagreeable to look at, but a graceful and beautiful swan. To be born in a duck's nest, in a farmyard, is of no consequence to a bird, if it is hatched from a swan's egg. He now felt glad at having suffered sorrow and trouble, because it enabled him to enjoy so much better all the pleasure and happiness around him; for the great swans swam round the new-comer, and stroked his neck with their beaks, as a welcome.

Into the garden presently came some little children, and threw bread and cake into the water.

"See," cried the youngest, "there is a new one!" And the rest were delighted, and ran to their father and mother, dancing and clapping their hands, and shouting joyously, "There is another swan come; a new one has arrived."

Then they threw more bread and cake into the water, and said, "The new one is the most beautiful of all; he is so young and pretty." And the old swans bowed their heads before him. Then he felt quite ashamed, and hid his head under his wing; for he did not know what to do, he was so happy, and yet not at all proud. He had been persecuted and despised for his ugliness, and now he heard them say he was the most beautiful of all the birds. Even the elder-tree bent down its bows into the water before him, and the sun shone warm and bright. Then he rustled his feathers, curved his slender neck, and cried joyfully, from the depths of his heart, "I never dreamed of such happiness as this." 1

---

1 English Translation: H.P. Paull (1872) in the Public Domain

The Sword in the Stone

It happened that Uther Pendragon, King of the Britons, died without leaving a male heir to succeed him. Actually this was not true, for Merlin the magician had advised him:

"When Queen Igraine bears your son, I shall carry him to safety. His name shall be Arthur. In my cave is a magnificent table that would have helped you to be a great king. Instead Arthur shall have it. And the whole world shall know of King Arthur and the Knights of the Round Table."

Now the barons in Briton were fighting among themselves, and foreign barbarians threatened to invade the realm. Merlin realized Arthur's time had come. So he called the barons to meet on Christmas Day at the great cathedral of London. When they arrived this was what they found: a gleaming sword thrust into an anvil that stood over a huge stone. And on the blade of the sword in letters of gold was written:

"Whoso pulleth out this sword of this stone is rightwise King of Briton."

Since none of the barons could move the sword even a hairsbreadth, jousting tournaments would be held. The winners would gain the chance to draw the sword from the stone. The baron Sir Ector sent his son to compete—the knight Sir Kay. Naturally Sir Kay brought his faithful squire along, who was his younger brother named Wart. But on the day of the tournament Sir Kay forgot— of all things—his sword.

"Wart, go to the inn and bring back a sword," Sir Kay requested. Wart obeyed immediately. Unable to find a sword, however, he happily remembered the sword in the stone. Lightly Wart grasped the hilt. He pulled it out easily!

Now when Sir Kay recognized the beautiful sword, he took it to Sir Ector and declared:

"Father, here is the sword from the stone! I must be king!"

Nevertheless, the wise father questioned Sir Kay, who then confessed that Wart had pulled the sword from the stone. Sir Ector knelt down before Wart and swore his loyalty:

"I am at your service, Arthur, High King of all Briton."

Then Sir Ector told Arthur the whole story about his real name, who his father had been, and why he had raised Arthur in secret. The other barons did not wish to humble themselves to a fifteen-year-old boy, however. Again and again Arthur had to plunge the sword into the stone and pull it out, until finally the jealous barons submitted. Then Merlin's words all came true. Arthur was knighted. He was crowned. He was King of Briton.

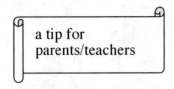
The Unit VI
11 x 17 Tri-Fold*

This is an *optional* Unit VI tool that might help 1) students who struggle with too many books and pieces of paper on small desks or 2) students whose large handwriting doesn't fit on the blanks provided in this book. Teachers with many students in your classrooms, before you attempt to take your class through these steps, do them once yourself.

You and each student will need an 11" x 17" piece of paper.

1. 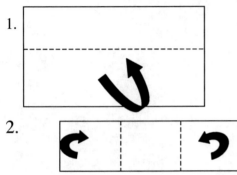   Fold the paper in half, "taco style" or like a hot dog bun. Crease.

2. 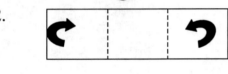   Next fold into thirds. Now you have almost a square. Crease firmly.

3. 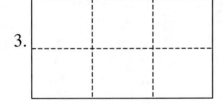   Unfold. Your page now has 6 areas.

4. 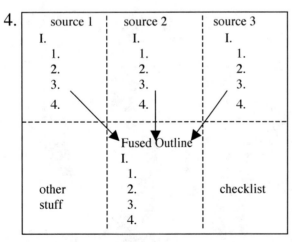   Spatially model the fused outline process like this.

*When teaching the fused outline from **2** source texts, you could use an 81/2" x 11" piece of paper. End up with 4 areas.

Odysseus and the Cyclops
Adapted from The Odyssey, by Homer

Returning home from the Trojan War, the Greek hero Odysseus and his men sailed to the island of the three Cyclopes. These were terrible giants who had one eye in the middle of their foreheads. They raised huge sheep, which they ate whole. Now Odysseus and his friends took shelter in the cave of the Cyclops named Polyphemus. When this monster came back later that night, he pushed a rock across the mouth of the cave. The men were completely trapped.

Odysseus planned their escape while the evil Cyclops slept. Then when morning arrived, the giant left to pasture his sheep. In haste Odysseus and his crew cut down an olive tree, which they sharpened and hid. Polyphemus asked Odysseus his name on that second night. "I am No One," answered Odysseus. "Have some wine!" The drink caused the monster to fall into a heavy sleep. Then the men easily climbed onto his chest. With all their might thrust the stake into the giant's eye. In pain he screamed.

"Are you under attack?" asked his brothers.

And Polyphemus cried out, "No One has hurt me!"

On the third day the blind Cyclops let his enormous sheep out of the cave, one at a time. As they went by, Polyphemus stroked their fleece. He was trying to prevent the men from escaping, but he was outsmarted. From his ship Odysseus bellowed, "We have gotten out of your cave by strapping ourselves beneath the animals' bellies, Polyphemus! I am not No One! I am Odysseus! Remember it well!"

Rumpelstiltskin
Adapted from the Brothers Grimm

A poor miller's daughter found herself in the king's castle. She was there because her father had foolishly bragged to the king that she could spin straw into gold. Now the first night that the king ordered her to perform this impossible task, a strange, small man appeared. After the young girl gave him her necklace, this little man agreed to spin all the straw into gold. The next night the same thing happened. On the third night, the king promised to marry the girl if she could spin all the straw into gold—a whole roomful. And a third time the strange man offered to help her. But when the girl had nothing to give him as payment, the little man tricked her. The miller's daughter agreed to give him her firstborn child once she became the queen. Indeed, by the next year a child was born, and the strange man came back to claim the baby. Oh, how the queen pleaded with him. So the tricky little man told her, "You have three days' time to guess my name. If you can guess it, you can keep the child."

The queen stayed up all night making a long list of all the common names she could think of. Was it Alex, Brian, Chris or David, Ed or Frank? She tried names from A to Z. "No, no," cried the short man to all the names. "Only two more days!"

The next day the worried young queen sent servants into the country to discover other names. When the troublesome little man came back, she read her long list of unusual names. Was it Gerald, Hercules, Inigo or Jocko, Kermit or

Leon? She tried names from A to Z. "No, no, and no again," cried the horrid, small man. "Only one more day!"

The desperate queen sent all of her servants to search high and low for Biblical names. By chance one servant did come upon the strange elf-man. He was dancing around a campfire in the forest and singing, "No one knows my wicked game. Rumpelstiltskin is my name." Quickly the servant raced home to report. The queen was overjoyed. She prepared her list of Biblical names from A to Q. Was it Matthew, Nathaniel, Obadiah or Peter? The tricky little man grinned and kept shaking his head.

He began to reach for the baby when the queen asked if his name was Rumpelstiltskin. The small, angry man was amazed. He yelled and pounded the table. He was so furious that he stomped right through the floor and disappeared. The royal family never saw him again. They lived happily ever after.

Bibliography

Baldwin, James. *Old Greek Stories*. New York: American Book Company. 1895.

Bloom, Richard. "#2751. A Primer on Verbs." December 2002. <http://teachers.net/

lessons/posts/2751.html> October 2007.

Bolt, Ranjit. *The Hare and the Tortoise and Other Fables of LaFontaine*.

Cambridge, Massachusetts: Barefoot Books. 2006.

"*Brothers Grimm*." November 2007. <http://wikipedia.org/wiki/Brothers_Grimm>

November 2007.

Bulfinch, Thomas. *Bulfinch's Mythology*. New York: Dell. 1959.

D'Aulaire, Ingri and Edgar Parin. *D'Aulaires' Book of Greek Myths*. New York: Bantam

Doubleday Dell Publishing Group, Inc. 1962.

Day, David. *The Search for King Arthur*. New York: Facts on File, Inc. 1995.

"Establishment of the Round Table." 2002.

<http://www.2020site.org/kingarthur/roundtable.html> October 2007.

Frost, Abigail. *Myths and Legends of the Age of Chivalry*. New York:

Marshall Cavendish. 1990.

"German Ballonists [sic] Mark Flight from East Germany." September 2004.

<http://www.russianatlanta.net/forums/post/7253.aspx> October 2007.

Gibson, Michael. *Gods, Men and Monsters From the Greek Myths*. New York:

Peter Bedrick Books. 1991.

"Hans Christian Andersen-A Concise Biography." 2002.

November 2007.

Hawthorne, Nathaniel. *Tanglewood Tales*. London: J.M. Dent & Sons Ltd.: 1950.

Herzberg, Max J. *Myths and Their Meanings*. Boston: Allyn and Bacon. n.d.g.

Krock, Lexi. "Great Escapes Part 2."

> <http://www.pbs.org/wgbh/nova/naziprison/escapes2.html> October 2007.

Lang, Andrew, editor. *The Blue Fairy Book*. New Edition volume 1. New York:

> Longmans, Green and Co. 1920.

Magill, Frank N., editor. *Encyclopedia of World Authors*. Pasadena, California:

> Salem Press, Inc. 2004.

Nardo, Don. *Greek and Roman Mythology*. San Diego, California: Lucent Books. 1998.

"Public Domain Images." 2007. <http://karenswhimsy.com/public-domain-images/>

> September 2007.

Pudewa, Andrew. "What? or That!—Reflections on Reports." Fall 2000.

> <http://excellenceinwriting.com> November 2007.

Pudewa, Andrew. 2002.

Pudewa, Andrew. 2004.

Pudewa, Andrew et. al. Teaching Writing: Structure & Style. Atascadero, California:

> Institute for Excellence in Writing. 2000.

Pudewa, Andrew. *Tips & Tricks for Teaching through the Nine Units of Structure &*

> *Style*. Atascadero, California: Institute for Excellence in Writing. 2007.

Talbott, Hudson. *The Sword in the Stone*. New York: Books of Wonder. 1991.

Talbott, Hudson. *King Arthur and the Round Table*. New York: Books of Wonder. 1994.

Webster, James B. *Blended Structure & Style in Composition*. 2nd Edition. Atascadero,

> California: Institute for Excellence in Writing. 2007.

Links & Best-Loved

www.brittanica.com

http://hca.gilead.org.il/   site about Hans Christian Andersen

http://ancienthistory.about.com   large site for historical topics

www.wikipedia.org   free encyclopedic information

www.excellenceinwriting.com   seminar calendar, catalog, archived
newsletters, student samples, links, FAQs, lesson plans

http://www.promo.net/pg/   Project Gutenberg is the oldest
internet source for e-books & e-texts; free

Additional **Best-Loved Fables** in the Western Hemisphere:

The Crow & the Pitcher   The Hare & the Tortoise
The Fox & the Grapes   The Little Engine That Could
The Boy Who Cried Wolf

Additional **Best Loved Fairy Tales** by Hans Christian Andersen:

The Brave Tin Soldier   Thumbelina
The Snow Queen   The Emperor's New Suit
The Red Shoes   The Princess & the Pea
The Little Matchgirl   The Little Mermaid

Additional **Best Loved Myths** in the Western Hemisphere:

Atalanta & the Golden Apples   The Trojan Horse
Pandora's Box   Jason & the Golden Fleece
The Twelve Labors of Hercules
King Midas & the Golden Touch

Best-Loved Classics for children & youth as well as insights into teaching:

A Thomas Jefferson Education. by Oliver Van DeMille